BRITISH
RAILWAYS
ILLUSTRATED

ANNUAL No.9

The Annual that takes the *Bah! Humbug!* out of Christmas – or at least postpones it till January, after we've cashed your cheque. The only Annual that *really does* get delivered by reindeer. And if you bought it direct by post you'll know what we mean… We hope all our readers had a wonderful 2000, and will look forward to 2001 – a year which will be most notable, as we all know, for the fiftieth anniversary of 70000 BRITANNIA. You have to get things in perspective, after all.

PAGE 4
BULLEID Q1s
By E.S. Youldon

Faced with the need for more freight locomotives with wide route availability Bulleid, characteristically, rejected more of the existing Q 0-6-0s in favour of an 0-6-0 of his own making. By this time (the early 1940s) it might seem odd that the new, modern, freight locomotive chosen by one of the Big Four should be an 0-6-0. After all, by the end of the War the 0-6-0 as a type would be deemed thoroughly obsolete. Yet, though 2-6-0s of various power classes appeared everywhere, the ranks of the pre-1948 0-6-0 were so great that they only finally went into decline when steam itself began to be severely reduced. There could be no major industrial nation in which the railways relied so heavily on the humble 0-6-0. In this Bulleid's Q1, though in a sense out of date before it was invented was, at the same time, the very acme of the 0-6-0 on earth, and quite suited to life right to the end of steam, along with any Mogul ever invented. The contradictions of these extraordinary machines, ugly yet endearing are caught in this straightforward account, together with its marvellous range of pictures.

PAGE 22
KITSONS IN DERBYSHIRE

Industrial locomotives – and the little 47000 series of 0-4-0STs could be so described – could never lay claim to noble looks. They were workmanlike at best, and that is how we came to be so fond of them but in these particular engines what might loosely be termed 'style' gave up – indeed went into reverse.

PAGE 24
SWINDON WORKS AND ITS PLACE IN…
Notes, Observations, Pictures and Undisguised Longings for Times Past by Paul Wilmshurst

A celebration of this great locomotive works, based on the repeated official account as developed over the years in a series of descriptive booklets, from *Swindon Works and its Place in Great Western History* in 1935, to *Swindon Works and its Place in British Railway History*, of 1950. 'BR' in this latter version, naturally, hardly got a mention…

PAGE 36
FOURUM
MONTROSE SCORCHER

PAGE 38
A WHILE LONGER AT THREE BRIDGES
A day out at the perfect engine shed.

PAGE 44
SNOW HILL INTERIORS
The ancient but amiable ghost of Snow Hill, Michael Mensing, caught every mood of this wonderful, doomed, station.

PAGE 46
A ROYAL SOVEREIGN
It was naturally impossible to have a Royal engine named after a football team (unless it was ARSENAL of course) and so it was that MANCHESTER CITY, chosen for royal work, was transformed into ROYAL SOVEREIGN, pride of Cambridge shed.

PAGE 48
THIRTIES FILE
LMS Racers
PRINCESS ELIZABETH on its record-breaking run of 16 November 1935, and the LMS toy with racehorses as a PR device. In the end they seem to have left that to the other lot…

PAGE 50
NEW SIGNAL BOX AT STAFFORD
Horribly ugly, the new Stafford box (a herald of many worse things to come unfortunately) was nevertheless doubtless appreciated by the blokes: '*it has been constructed in accordance with agreed modern standards with brick walls faced with hand made bricks,* [!] *reinforced concrete roof and wide vision metal windows. The building is centrally heated by a thermostatically controlled gas fire boiler and is equipped with modern electric lighting.*'

PAGE 52
FOURUM
Changes in the Life of GLASGOW HIGHLANDER

PAGE 54
VANISHED TRADE
Coal, and why it went.

PAGE 56
CENTREPIECE
High summer at Kings Cross.

PAGE 58
URCHIN TALES
Or: Shame About the Photographs, Just Smell the Steam
By Graham Onley
More from this merry band of platform enders, condemned forever to support Northampton Town F.C.

PAGE 60
DIESEL DAWN
Ugly Ducklings
The question of what happened to the men who drew out the design for the Kitson and LM 0-4-0STs was answered at last when some of the Hudswell Clarke, North British and Barclay small diesel shunters began appearing in the 1950s. The bewildering variety of diesels that BR ended up with, and their inevitable early demise which later attracted such opprobrium for BR, was not a situation of the railways's making. It came about largely through the political need to spread the largesse around. Where it affected most of us of course, at the level of the Ian Allan ABC, these weighty affairs mattered not at all – the more obscure classes to chase the better!

PAGE 64
STATION SURVEY
A TALE OF TWO WELWYNS
By 'Oliver Bury'
Return of the popular feature *Station Survey*. This time two stations in one, from the original and rather snooty 'Welwyn' on the hill to the brash Johnny-come-lately down below – the 'Garden City'.

PAGE 80
WAR REPORT
The Army Auxiliary Pioneer Corps in France
A remarkable series of official postcards, issued for morale boosting, though the price of a shilling probably inhibited the distribution somewhat.

PAGE 84
TWO SCOTS ON BUSHEY TROUGHS
Late in the day, two Royal Scots forge north in time-honoured style.

PAGE 86
NO SMOKE WITHOUT FIRE…

PAGE 88
BUCHAN AND BEYOND
Notes by Bryan Wilson
Travel the St Combs branch and other lonely parts of the far North East with Michael Bland in September 1958.

PAGE 96
ENDPIECE
Intimate Portrait of a Pannier Tank.

You'll Remember those Black and White Days…

Photograph front cover. 70032 TENNYSON at Longsight shed 15 March 1953, being cleaned for its naming ceremony. M.N. Bland, The Transport Treasury.

Photograph rear cover. S15 4-6-0 30839 on a winter's day at Waterloo about 1963, the cold air betraying every steam leak. J.G. Walmsley, The Transport Treasury.

Photograph this page. Keeping an eye out at Liverpool Street. Photograph Jack Kirke.

EDITORIAL MATTERS
Contributions, submissions, photographs or whatever (remember the contributor must address and attend to copyright), readers' letters, bouquets and brickbats for **British Railways Illustrated** must be addressed to Editor, **Chris Hawkins** at 59A, High Street, Clophill, Bedfordshire MK45 4BE E-mail Chris@irwellpressmags.demon.co.uk Tel.01525 861888 or Fax. 01525 861888 or Printed & Bound by The Amadeus Press, Huddersfield Copyright :- Irwell Press 2000

IRWELL PRESS
No.1 in Railway Publishing

BULLEID Q1s

By E.S. YOULDON

CONCEPT

When Oliver Bulleid surveyed the Southern Railway's freight scene in the early days of the Second World War, he concluded that additional freight locomotives with wide route availability were required. An 0-6-0 design was preferred but the existing Q class of 1938, the nearest contender, was rejected on the grounds of limited boiler capacity Straightforward enlargement of the Q was ruled out because the result would have been an engine too heavy for the wide range of route envisaged. So Bulleid designed a powerful 0-6-0 using the Lord Nelson pattern throat and backplate for the firebox. A firegrate area of 27sq.ft. bettered the Q figure by 23 per cent and a firebox heating surface of 170sq.ft. by 39 per cent.

In spite of such formidable enhancement the new engine, to be known as the Q1 class, weighed in at only 51 tons 5 cwt., a mere 1 ton 15 cwt. over the far smaller Maunsell predecessor. This achievement was obtained by eliminating non-essential running plates and splashers, the use of sheet metal instead of platework where possible, extensive welding and lightweight frame members. Boiler lagging was a type known as 'Idaglass' – a brand chosen because it was available in the UK; its drawback was that it wasn't capable of supporting a load. The boiler and firebox casing therefore had to be independently mounted giving rise to the unique telescopic styling that, essentially, had to follow the cross section of the firebox. The overall result was a powerful 0-6-0 that could traverse 93 per cent of the Southern's route mileage.

An early complaint from the footplate was that the sight just below of a coupling rod whirling around was unnerving in view of the dire consequences in the event of a fracture. Bulleid's reply was that the protection afforded by the presence of a traditional running plate would be minimal should such a catastrophe occur. The complaint was heard no more! As a bonus, the absence of running plates and splashers meant that the inside motion was rendered more accessible.

Photograph right. 33013 in third rail territory in September 1959 with a lengthy goods in tow. Photograph The Transport Treasury.

EMERGENCE

In March 1942 the first of the class was unveiled and the visual appearance had the effect of a bombshell. To many observers this was the end of civilisation as they knew it and the Southern's sanity was questioned in a no uncertain manner! Over the years perception mellowed somewhat and enthusiasts accepted the Q1 as part of the Southern scene so that one of them adjacent, for instance, to a T9 was just another fascinating contrast among many that the Southern had to offer. There was in fact a plain innocence about the Q1 that was lacking in the 'show everything' culture of the Ivatt class 4 2-6-0 of 1947.

You'll Remember those Black and White Days...

DETAILS

Away from appearance, the Q1 had much that followed convention. Valve gears were Stephenson and the cylinders had outside admission piston valves above them, operated by rocking shafts. Merchant Navy features that were repeated included BFB (Bulleid Firth Brown) wheel centres, steam reverser and multiple

jet blastpipe and large diameter stovepipe chimney. Thermic syphons, oil baths and electric lighting, however, were all absent. The whistle was standard Southern. The six-wheeled tender of 3,700 gallons capacity was also of light construction; this would turn out to be a mixed blessing – see later. At the cab end the tenders were

provided with external sliding covers for wartime blackout; these survived until the end although invariably, as one would expect, they were pushed well back.

Ample cupboard room was provided for the enginemen, and an extension to the tender frontplate in line with the cab roof gave protection especially when running tender first.

No.C1 as finished, following adjustments to position of cab number and tender legend. Two handrails soon appeared on the front of the smokebox and one on the door itself. The three smokebox door lamp irons were later lowered.

The tender cab included water filling holes to save the fireman from clambering to the top. One problem was the very restricted standing space in front of the smokebox for shed staff when, for example, shovelling out ash. The expedient was sometimes adopted of placing a plank across the buffer housings – enough to give today's Health and Safety inspectors kittens!

BUILDING AND NUMBERS

Forty engines were built, all in 1942 and completion was divided equally between Brighton and Ashford Works, with the inevitable result that overall order of entry into traffic was out of harmony with number sequence. Running numbers were to have been 550 to 589 to follow the Q class and in consequence Adams A12 No.555 was to be renumbered

3555 to clear the way. However, second thoughts prevailed and the new 0-6-0s were blessed (some say cursed!) with the same form of identification as the Merchant Navy class by becoming C1 to C40 until renumbered 33001 to 33040 by BR in 1948-51.

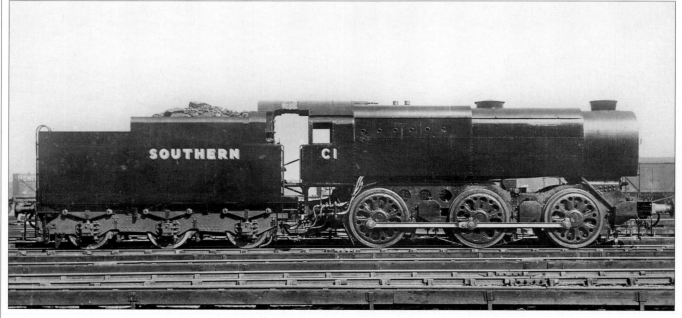

Side view of the prototype. Steam sanding to the front of the leading wheels and to both sides of the centre wheels. The pipe behind the rear wheels delivered a steam jet for rail cleaning, and gravity sanding on the front of the tender prevented tender wheels from 'picking up' in poor adhesion conditions. 'Picking up' was a term used when braking caused wheels to lock up and therefore skid. This could happen when rails were wet and the tender was relatively light – as it would be with say, coal and water low. The Q1 tender sander was then used when it was deemed prudent, such as with an unfitted freight in tow.

You'll Remember those Black and White Days...

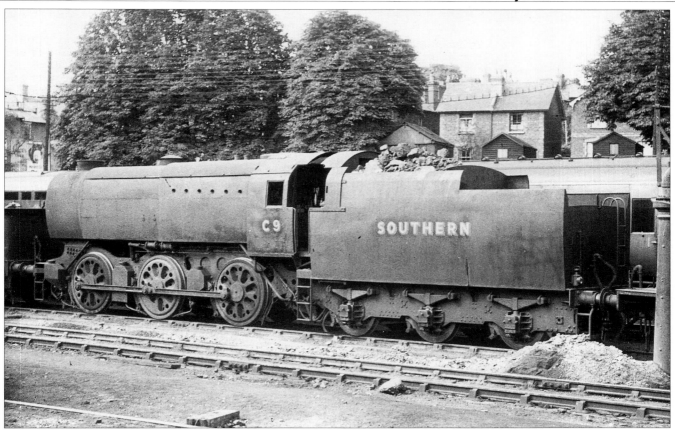

C9 at Guildford in August 1947, showing blackout cover at front of tender.

AT WORK

Whatever their looks the newcomers were soon appreciated as worthy workhorses for goods trains with a percentage of work on van and passenger trains. Early allocations (see table) involved few sheds with long runs at each. Gradually more sheds acquired Q1s and running

numbers became scattered. Away from the top links there were few limits to the range of trains the Q1s could haul or to where they could operate. One drawback was the light construction of the tender, which imposed a restriction on the weight of an unfitted freight that could be controlled on a falling gradient. The

S15 4-6-0 with a hefty bogie tender could, under test, stop a 70 wagon train in 740 yards less than C18 down Micheldever bank. A Q1 was accordingly a rare sight west of Salisbury, though odd appearances were known as far down the line as Okehampton. One once notably appeared at Exeter GW shed when

33037 at Paddock Wood with the 12.16pm Tonbridge to Maidstone West on 27 May 1961. Photograph John Scrace.

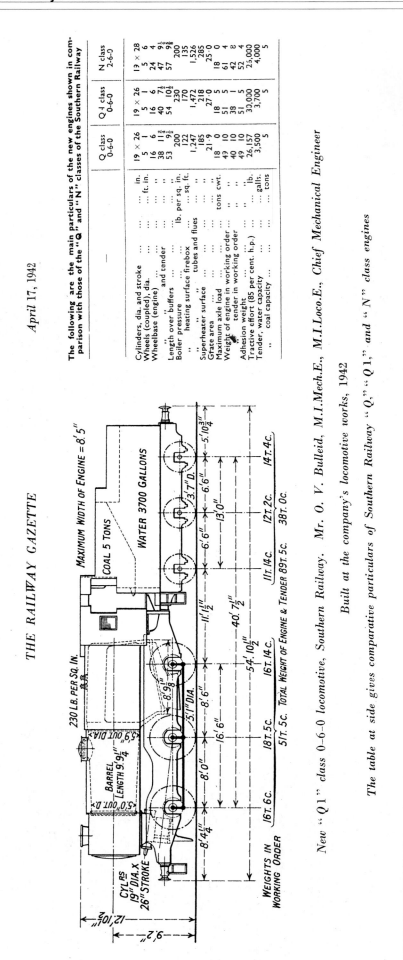

THE RAILWAY GAZETTE

April 17, 1942

The following are the main particulars of the new engines shown in comparison with those of the "Q" and "N" classes of the Southern Railway

		Q class 0-6-0	Q1 class 0-6-0	N class 2-6-0
Cylinders, dia. and stroke	... in.	19 × 26	19 × 26	19 × 28
Wheels (coupled), dia.	... ft. in.	5 – 1	5 – 1	5 – 6
Wheelbase (engine)	...	16 – 6	16 – 6	24 – 4
" and tender	...	38 – 11¾	40 – 7¾	47 – 9¼
Length over buffers	...	53	54 – 10½	57
Boiler pressure	... lb. per sq. in.	200	230	200
Heating surface firebox	... sq. ft.	122	170	135
" tubes and flues	...	1,247	1,472	1,526
Superheater surface	...	185	218	285
Grate area	...	21.9	27.0	25.0
Maximum axle load	... tons cwt.	18 – 0	18 – 5	18 – 4
Weight of engine in working order	...	49 – 10	38 – 5	61 – 4
" tender in working order	...	40 – 10	51 – 5	42 – 8
Adhesion weight	...	49 – 10	51 – 5	52 – 4
Tractive effort (85 per cent. h.p.)	... lb.	26,157	33,000	25,000
Tender, water capacity	... galls.	3,500	3,700	4,000
" coal capacity	... tons	5	5	5

New "Q1" class 0-6-0 locomotive, Southern Railway. Mr. O. V. Bulleid, M.I.Mech.E., M.I.Loco.E., Chief Mechanical Engineer

Built at the company's locomotive works, 1942

The table at side gives comparative particulars of Southern Railway "Q," "Q1," and "N" class engines

the Exmouth Junction turntable was out of action.

BR power classification, applied to the cabsides from the mid-fifties, was 5FA. It should here be mentioned that the Southern refined certain of the permitted freight loading categories into A and B with A being the less restrictive.

Overhaul of the Q1s was mainly undertaken by Ashford Works with occasional visits to Eastleigh until mid-1961 when the latter assumed full responsibility.

MODIFICATIONS

Changes were on a small scale. A mechanical lubricator for cylinders and steamchests driven from the leading left-hand crankpin featured from new on C14 to C16, and C29 to C40. A similar lubricator was added later to sixteen others but nine, Nos.33005, 33011, 33019, 33022, 33023, 33024, 33025, 33026 and 33028 never, as far as can be gathered from photographs, were thus endowed. In the case of 33013, 33017 and 33036 a second mechanical lubricator was added for supplying the axleboxes.

AWS gear was fitted – sometimes incomplete – to most of the class from 1959. Less visible changes were strengthened smokebox, smokebox door and tender tank, all of which must have dented the original lightweight concept to a limited extent.

LIVERY

Plain black was the only livery applied to the Q1s. After nationalisation just one engine, C11, bore the interim 'S' prefix. On receiving their new numbers some of the class retained SOUTHERN on the tender whereas others had BRITISH RAILWAYS in southern sunshine style. There were several other intermediate versions but from around mid-1949 the situation had settled down with Gill Sans cabside number and first BR emblem on the tender in the large version; this was applied to all of the class. The second BR emblem was first seen on the class in its large version and later in the small size, but came too late to appear on all Q1s.

EXPERIMENTS

In late 1944 Bulleid was keen to experiment with tender first working on a large scale – doubtless because at the time the SR planned to replace elderly tanks on branch lines by a modern class. So a series of proposals was drawn up which included one based on the Q1 with special consideration for reversible running. No.C26 was selected but had its tender replaced by one from a batch of new West Country tenders that were stored awaiting completion

You'll Remember those Black and White Days...

33038 at Feltham on 3 June 1962. Mechanical lubricator ahead of and above leading wheel. Photograph R.A. Panting.

of engines. It gave better rearwards vision, so a new 4,500 gallon Pacific tender, No.3256, was painted black and attached to the Q1 from December 1944 until August 1945.

In September 1945 No.C36 was given duplicate controls on the right-hand side and was then paired with 3256, running with it until April 1946 and covering 10,170 miles. Trials included high speed runs in reverse between Ashford and Maidstone but though the dual control arrangement did not prove satisfactory a diagram, drawing No.W6393, was produced for a reversible form of Q1.

Nothing more took place in this direction and C36 reverted to standard condition and tender 3256 was repainted and at last went to the

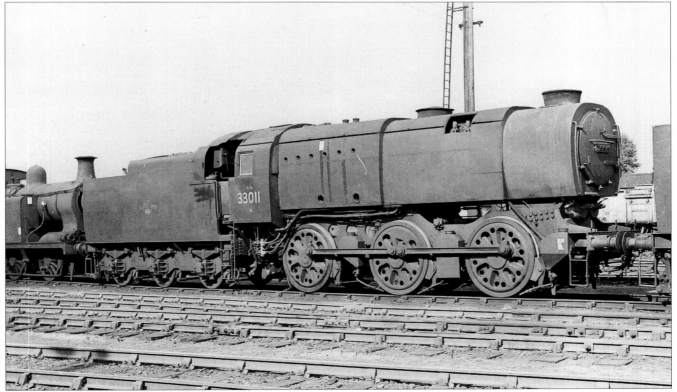

33011 at Eastleigh shed on 27 August 1963. The discarded casing section reveals twin boiler feeds. Second BR emblem, small version. Photograph John Scrace.

right kind of engine (current terminology!) by attachment to new Pacific No.21C138 in September 1946. Further trials were in any case rendered unnecessary because the modern tank project had moved on to more sophisticated levels and finally blossomed in 1949 in the shape of the Leader – but that as they say is another story. In the fullness of time salvation came to the Southern Region, as far as a modern tank was concerned, with the LMR and Standard 2-6-2 and 2-6-4 tank classes in the 1950s.

Acknowledgements:

Bulleid of the Southern by H.A.V. Bulleid (Ian Allan 1977) was consulted and assistance was provided by Barry Fletcher, Peter Cupper and the RCTS.

LOCO	BUILT	WHERE BUILT	330XX APPLIED	FIRST SHED	SHED 7/53	LAST SHED	WDN
C1	3/42	BRIGHTON	10/50†	GFD	GFD	GFD	5/64
C2	5/42	"	12/48	"	"	FEL	7/63
C3	"	"	1/51	"	"	FEL	6/64
C4	6/42	"	10/48†	"	"	GFD	1/65
C5	"	"	11/48	"	"	GFD	6/63
C6	"	"	3/50	"	FEL	"	1/66
C7	7/42	"	5/50†	"	"	FEL	1/64
C8	"	"	7/50†	"	"	FEL	8/63
C9	"	"	5/50	"	"	9E	9/65
C10	9/42	"	11/49	"	"	FEL	1/64
C11*	"	"	12/50	ELH	"	FEL	8/63
C12	"	"	1/50	"	"	GFD	11/64
C13	10/42	"	7/50†	"	"	FEL	7/63
C14	"	"	4/49	"	HG	GFD	1/64
C15	11/42	"	3/50	"	"	GFD	11/64
C16	"	"	3/50	"	"	3B	8/63
C17	5/42	ASHFORD	12/49	"	ELH	3B	1/64
C18	4/42	"	5/49†	"	BAT	9E	7/65
C19	5/42	"	5/48	"	"	GFD	12/63
C20	"	"	4/50	"	ELH	GFD	1/66
C21	6/42	"	11/50†	FEL	"	ELH	8/63
C22	"	"	2/50	"	BAT	GFD	1/64
C23	"	"	11/48	"	ELH	ELH	6/64
C24	"	"	3/49	"	"	3B	8/63
C25	7/42	"	5/48	"	"	GFD	7/63
C26	"	"	3/49†	"	TON	9E	9/65
C27	"	"	6/48	"	"	GFD	1/66
C28	8/42	"	10/48	"	"	3B	2/63
C29	"	"	3/50	"	"	3B	1/64
C30	9/42	"	7/48	"	"	FEL	6/64
C31	10/42	"	6/49	"	"	3B	9/63
C32	11/42	"	12/48	"	"	GFD	1/64
C33	"	"	7/48	"	"	GFD	6/64
C34	"	"	4/49	"	"	GFD	1/64
C35	12/42	"	4/48	"	"	GFD	6/64
C36	"	"	10/48	"	"	GFD	"
C37	"	BRIGHTON	6/48	"	HG	ELH	10/63
C38	"	"	12/48	"	ELH	FEL	1/64
C39	"	"	12/48	"	STL	ELH	6/64
C40	"	"	6/48	"	"	FEL	"

* Ran as SC11 from 1/48 until 12/50
† Cannot be precisely determined, but accurate within one month either way
(All cut up on withdrawal except for C1 which survives on the Bluebell Railway)

33040 on coal empties ex-Tolworth, at Wimbledon on 6 June 1964. Photograph Alec Swain, The Transport Treasury.

* Ran as SC11 from 1/48 until 12/50
† Cannot be precisely determined, but accurate within one month either way
(All cut up on withdrawal except for C1 which survives on the Bluebell Railway)

You'll Remember those Black and White Days...

33020 at Nine Elms on 4 September 1965. It has AWS gear and carries the second BR emblem, the large version. Photograph Alec Swain, The Transport Treasury.

33036 at Guildford – one of the Q1s with twin mechanical lubricators. Steam reverser leaking somewhat. Photograph N. Hamshere.

33027 at Kingston on a van train. Towards the end casing covers got removed and often lost!

No.C18, the first turned out by Ashford. Note the short-lived pattern of front vertical handrail. A commendable feature of Bulleid's engines was the placing of the cab footsteps centrally with the opening.

C24 at Bournemouth shed in 1948. Its smokebox door awaits the horizontal rail. Photograph The Transport Treasury.

33004 has a quiet smoke in Havant Yard on 12 September 1949. Renumbered in Southern numerals but not re-lettered. Photograph R.H. Fullagar, The Transport Treasury.

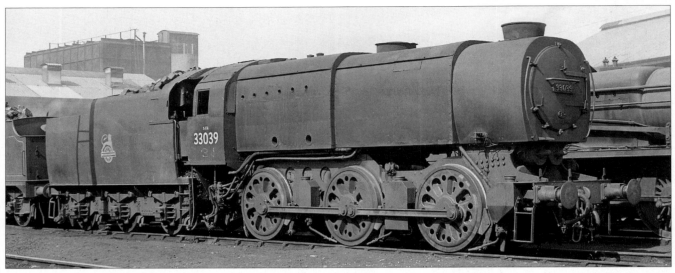

33039 at Hither Green shed on 27 April 1958 shows the first BR emblem well. 5FA classification visible on cabside. Photograph Peter Groom.

33027 at Feltham shed on 29 May 1960. AWS equipment in front of, and underneath, cab. Photograph Peter Groom.

33012 at Feltham shed on 15 October 1960. Photograph Peter Groom.

'S Q1s

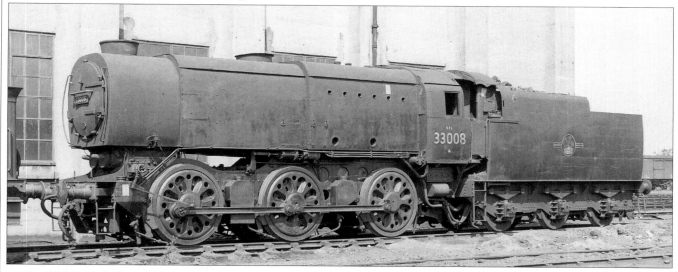

33008 at Feltham shed on 15 August 1963. Overhead catenary warning label on leading sandbox and firebox casing. Photograph Peter Groom.

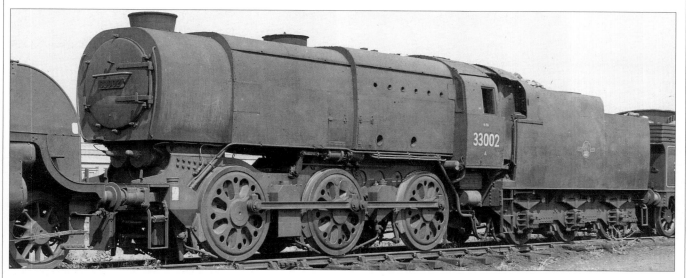

33002 in store at Feltham shed, 15 August 1963. Photograph Peter Groom.

33010 in store at Feltham shed on 7 April 1964. Two access doors open above steam reverser. Cabside window visible (originally unglazed) and a visor has been added. Photograph Peter Groom.

Top left opposite page. 33034 shows its smokebox contents. From the top: Petticoat into which the brake ejector also discharges; live steampipes to cylinders left and right; superheater elements; blastpipe nozzles with blower ring. To open this type of door meant loosening a number of clamps but the arrangement had the advantage of giving unimpeded access without having to remove a hefty crossbar. Photograph The Transport Treasury.

Top right opposite page. 33034 has had its piston valves removed – all the signs, in fact, of a withdrawn loco being robbed. The lower centre lamp iron on a Q1 was slightly offset to the right to miss a platform bolt. Photograph The Transport Treasury.

Above. 33008 at Guildford shed with a backdrop of Adams goods and cattle wagons. Photograph B.H. Fletcher, The Transport Treasury.

Bottom left. 33015 at Guildford shed being raked out over the pits. Photograph The Transport Treasury.

33019 at Reading (Southern) shed in July 1952. Above the intermediate sandbox can be seen the bearing for the reverser cross shaft, the connection for which can be glimpsed on the far side under the casing. Note frame lightening holes between middle and rear wheels. Photograph The Transport Treasury.

33031 at Ashford shed on 3 August 1957. The hinged cover for access above the steam reverser is clearly visible. Photograph The Transport Treasury.

33039 at St. Leonards shed on 9 August 1956. This one (and others too) has *two* hinged access covers above its reverser. Another of the Southern's endearing contrasts is provided by the 'L' 4-4-0 alongside. Photograph J. Robertson, The Transport Treasury.

33040 comes off the turntable at St. Leonards shed on 9 August 1956 clean enough to clearly show the first BR emblem. Photograph J. Robertson, The Transport Treasury.

C23 outside Ashford Works on 7 June 1947 with its boiler cladding removed and clothing pulled away to reveal the single ring barrel and dome. The two feed pipes have been removed and the blast pipe reposes on the front platform. It was not unusual at Ashford for the 'lighter' jobs to be done outside and engines could also be 'finished off' outside – it was something to do with targets and bonuses! Photograph H.C. Casserley.

Kitsons in Derbyshire

Painfully ungainly but somehow endearing, the 47000 series of ten 0-4-0STs, the first five built by Kitson for the LMS and the later ones by BR at Horwich, led a retiring life, like others of their ilk. On many different railways specialised, short wheelbase engines such as these, by their nature spent their lives secreted away in harbours and works, lurking in impenetrable docks and breweries. In the case of 47007 its hideaway, from January 1959 at least, was the remote Cromford and High Peak, at Sheep Pasture. 47004, one of the earlier five, had the smaller bunker and larger tank of the first batch (see *Railway Bylines*, Vol.2 No.3 for a complete account of these curious beasts). In these first three pictures, 47007 is at Sheep Pasture shed (its remains are seen above – just walls and a floor, for it blew down in a gale in 1962). The shed, famous for a *grid reference* entry in *The Shed Directory*, was characterised by the home-made but extremely efficient water tank-cum-column. The whole thing was far more sophisticated than any lowland equivalent – note the white disc for instance, which is a level indicator.

The picture of 47004 (bottom) was actually taken at Hasland shed which (even with railway terraces provided close by) had a sort of moorland setting almost reminiscent of the C&HP. 47004 went there for some obscure works shunt in 1936 and stayed (though it was frequently loaned out) to the end in 1964. 47007 (which had also had a brief spell at Hasland in the 1950s) was withdrawn a few weeks earlier, at the end of 1963. Note the ornate brackets (opposite page) for fire irons on the right-hand side of 47007's tank; 47004 and the rest of the earlier series had them too but higher up – one can just be glimpsed beyond its open filler cap. There was not much room on these things, and the square box on the back of the cab is the tool/ oil bottle locker for the crew. The 25kV stickers are hardly inappropriate of course but 'orders were orders'. Note, lastly, the deflector plates on 47007's bunker. These are not lids to the coal boxes, as might be imagined at first but are just that – deflectors to stop coal dropping between the bunker and the boiler. Happy engine-picking!

SWINDON WORKS AND ITS PLACE IN...

Some Notes, Observations, Pictures and Undisguised Longings for Times Past by Paul Wilmshurst

An odd title but one firmly in a tradition of celebrating this great locomotive works. At least three substantial booklets – and there were almost certainly more – were published with the same title. *Swindon Works and its Place in Great Western History* came in 1935, *Swindon Works GWR* in 1947 (inside it carried the same title *Swindon Works and its Place in Great Western History*) while the very same text (with different illustrations) was published again under BR auspices in 1950, entitled *Swindon Works and its Place in British Railway History*. 'BR' in this version hardly got a mention.

Swindon was in a way perhaps the most shocking of the works closures, startling because not only had it ranked among the greatest of the big four along with Doncaster, Crewe and the rest but because for so long it had enjoyed such a

With so many furnaces, forges and hearths, Swindon literally bristled with smokestacks of one form or another. Here is the view across the main line about 1912, looking north through the chimneys of what became the Sawmill. The buildings opposite are the forerunners of the new 'A' Shop – the Fitting and Machine Shops ('R' on the plan). The old building in front of it, parallel to the running line, was once the engine shed, opened in 1842 with the coming of the railway and subsequently incorporated into the works. The later engine shed, on the Gloucester line, opened in 1871 and the old shed seems to have been used only for the dwindling numbers of broad gauge locos after that. In was finally abandoned for this purpose in 1892 of course, and was eventually demolished in 1930. In 1912, it was obviously the accepted place to put old smokebox doors!

complete primacy on its own system – the GW and the WR after it.

So it seemed that a short photographic tribute to the great works, with a modest account lending from this venerable series of booklets, might be appropriate...

'Swindon – the town on the hill – dates back at least eight centuries...' This was the opening sentence of all the booklets down the years and was still used in a 1970s pamphlet for an 'open day' tour of the works. So let's

start with it again... Swindon, a town sited on a hill – unremarkably for southern England – did indeed date back some 800 years, though much the same could be said of many settlements in the country. What had propelled it to railway engineering fame was its chance location in the middle of Brunel's great project, roughly half way between London and Bristol. The Great Western had arrived in 1840 and the line through to Bristol was complete the following year.

The great 'A' Shop, fairly new in 1908, looking west from the water tower/tank with the main line on the left. The second part of the shop, with its sixty 100ft. pits, has yet to be built, on the far end of this original building – it had roof pitches quite different from the earlier building. All the staff are carefully posing for the long-exposure photograph including one stalwart standing boldly atop the smokebox of the 2-4-0. The building immediately in front of the new 'A' shop and separated from it by the traverser, was the stripping shed. Note the dumb-buffered wagon in the foreground – this marks it for internal use only.

The writer of the original guidebook had the advantage of access to the GW's vast and punctiliously-kept archive, and recorded in fascinating detail Gooch's early travails with locomotives. Extracts such as this tell the story: *'I was much engaged up to the end of May in getting all* *ready for opening the portion of the Great Western Railway from London to Maidenhead. On the 31st May 1838, the directors made their first trip over the whole length of this portion, and it was opened to the public on the 4th June, and then my difficulties with the engines began. The 'North Star' and the six from the Vulcan* *Foundry Company were the only ones I could at all depend upon. For many weeks my nights were spent in a carriage in the engine-house at Paddington, as repairs had to be done to the engines at night to get them to do their work next day. The 'North Star', being the most powerful one and in other respects the best, was*

A similar view around 1947, showing the even larger extension to the shops (with their different roof pitches) at the far end. The loco boiler and its chimney have gone from the stripping shed and many more spurs have appeared round the turntable. A 72XX 2-8-2T, No.7247 ex-works, sits in the centre of the view. The new shelter is the engine reception building – for dropping fires, taking coal out, draining boilers and so on.

GREAT WESTERN RAILWAY MAGAZINE

Just a Hundred Years Ago

How Choice fell upon Swindon

IT was a few months more than a century ago, on October 6, 1840, to be precise, that the Directors of the Great Western Railway resolved "That the Company's principal Locomotive Station and Repairing Shops be established at or near the junction with the Great Western Union Railway at Swindon." That resolution was the result of a carefully-considered report made by Gooch to his chief, Brunel, on September 13, 1840, in which he gave sound and convincing reasons for his choice of site.

The provision of a central repair depot for locomotives was by then becoming a matter of some urgency, for negotiations were in hand for leasing both the Bristol and Exeter, and the Cheltenham and Great Western Union Railway, the latter planned to join the Great Western Railway at Swindon. Another consideration was the fact that delivery of the hundred-odd standard type engines, built to Gooch's designs by outside contractors, was progressing steadily, and the engine stock was thus increasing month by month.

Brunel decided to discuss Gooch's recommendation on the site, and it is an unauthenticated but quite understandable story that the Chief Engineer and his young "Superintendent of Locomotive Engines" made something of an outing of the occasion. They are said to have lunched in the open fields near the spot where the Cheltenham line was to join the Great Western below the little Wiltshire market town on the hill. Brunel appears to have been impressed with points which had influenced Gooch's selection and to have fully concurred. In fixing the exact location they decided to throw a stone, or maybe a sandwich, from where they were lunching, and where it should fall to drive in a peg, marking the site of the future locomotive depot. This method of arriving at a decision hardly savours of the precision of a Brunel or a Gooch, but it can pass as a story. After all, these very human young men (their united ages were about 58) after disposing of their main problem and their lunch, may well have agreed to mark their decision in the boylike way recorded.

The recommendation for the provision of a central locomotive depot at Swindon was duly confirmed by the Directors at their meeting on February 25, 1841, when it was decided "to provide an engine establishment commeasurate with the wants of the Company, where a change of engines may be advantageously made and the trains stopped for the passengers taking refreshment . . ." No mention was made of an intention to build new locomotives, and apparently the policy of having engines built by contractors to Great Western design was then regarded as quite satisfactory.

The repair shops were commenced forthwith and were partly working in 1842, although they were not in full operation until the following January. The running shed was first brought into use with a staff of about 100.

It will have been observed that the Directors had in mind the stopping of all trains at Swindon for a change of engines, and coupled with this stop was the question of providing refreshment facilities for passengers. It is to be regretted that the Directors of that day were not so far-seeing in the matter of "re-fuelling" the passengers as of providing for their loco-

motives. There were special considerations, however, and it was in order to keep down capital expenditure that the contractors who built the engine depot, Messrs. J. & C. Rigby, were allowed to construct the new Swindon Junction station and refreshment rooms at their own expense, and to remunerate themselves by catering for passengers at the station. This they agreed to do on the undertaking that all trains should stop at Swindon "for a reasonable period of about ten minutes" for refreshments for passengers, and that there should be no rival catering establishment on the railway between London and Bristol.

These arrangements were embodied in a lease to run for 99 years from Christmas, 1841, at a rent of a penny a year, and within one week of the completion of the lease the astute builders had sublet the refreshment business for seven years at a rent of £1,100 per annum and a premium of £6,000! When that lease had expired they sold it outright for £20,000. The refreshment arrangements were never entirely satisfactory while in contractors' hands, and there were many complaints from the travelling public which put the Company in a difficult position. After an unsuccessful lawsuit brought by the contractor, who maintained that certain mail-trains should stop at Swindon in accordance with the general arrangement, the business changed hands in 1875 at £45,000. From this date it may be inferred that the refreshment business at Swindon was for some time either static or diminishing; in any case, when the contractor disposed of the undertaking five years later, it was for £10,000 less than the price he paid for it. But what magic was possessed by the new purchaser, who after holding it for only a year, sold it in 1881 for £70,000—a profit of 100 per cent!

To the Great Western Railway itself the unlucky contract of 1841 had been anything but "refreshing," and brought only increasing difficulties in its train. After 45 years, therefore, the Company "took the bull by the horns" and brought the contract to an end. It cost no less than £100,000 to get rid of what from the start had proved to be an incubus and a strangle-hold on traffic work, due to the enforced stoppages at Swindon over a period when the Company was building up a great reputation for the speed of its trains to and from the West of England.

It is appropriate to this article to record that the contractors who built the engine depot, station and refreshment rooms, also constructed the first cottages for the Company's workmen. This was the start of New Swindon, which went steadily from strength to strength as the years passed and the Great Western works extended.

Both Brunel and Gooch were far-seeing men who believed in an expanding future for railways, and the Great Western Railway in particular, but it is doubtful if even they, speculating a hundred years ago upon the provision of a central locomotive depot at Swindon, visualised the huge industrial plant which in less than a century was to cover well over 300 acres, find work for 12,000 employees, and multiply the population of the little town about twenty-six times, to the total of 65,000.—W. G. CHAPMAN.

You'll Remember those Black and White Days...

The Swindon Stock Shed, a peculiar institution (Horwich had something similar) which seemed to exist merely to store locomotives that were not immediately required elsewhere. A case in point concerned the 2-8-0Ts built during the Depression; they seem to have been ordered to 'keep the works going' and finding no work they went straight into store in the Stock Shed, only emerging for conversion to 2-8-2Ts. The outside frame pannier tank is No.1282 and the 4-4-0 No.3359 TREGEAGLE, with an ROD 2-8-0 behind.

my chief reliance, but she was often getting into trouble from other causes.'

It was clear that a large repairing centre would soon be needed; Gooch duly investigated the various towns and villages on the main line and, he records, *'on full consideration I reported in favour of Swindon, it being the junction with the Cheltenham branch and also a convenient division of the Great Western line for engine working. Mr Brunel and I went to look at the ground, then only green fields, and he agreed with me as to it being the best place.'*

From this, an afternoon spent by Gooch and Brunel poking about in a few fields, grew Swindon Works. Significant dates abound in the story of Swindon and the Paddington public affairs section made sure they were properly remarked upon at the appropriate intervals. In the dark time of January 1941 the *Great Western Magazine* could cheer everyone up by reference to the steady continuity of British life. It is clear also that the affair of the Swindon Refreshment Room, so intertwined in the origins of the works and yet not *so* familiar in GW lore, still smarted. *(see opposite)*

The Great Western was perhaps the first of the great companies to centralise all its repair operations; the carriage department had been suffering increasingly cramped and awkward conditions at Paddington and after the worthies of Oxford saw off a proposal to site a new C&W works in the university town, they were finally established at Swindon. Work began in the summer of 1867 and finished the following year. The first coaches built at Swindon went into service in 1869. Much of the

Great Western's time and effort later went into the reduction of its broad gauge to standard gauge and at its final end in 1892 more than thirteen miles of extra sidings had been put in at Swindon for the redundant stock. Favourite figures chosen to illustrate the influence of the railway on Swindon and its growth are as follows: in 1892, when the work of gauge conversion was at its height, the total employed at the works was nearly 10,000, and by 1948 was 12,000. In 1876 the figure had been only 4,500. Compare all this with the figure for the entire population of the town in 1841 – just 2,459.

Swindon repaired more than a hundred locomotives in a year by 1948, with a capacity for turning out two or three new locomotives a week. It was truly a mighty undertaking, drawing in all the multifarious raw

materials and turning out every device that could find a use on the railway, from locos and stock to the lowliest spare part for distribution all over the GW empire. In 1948 the various departments in Swindon Works were listed as here, and the reference letters can (by and large) be related to the plan.

A	Erectors, Boilermakers, Painters, Machine and Wheel Shop
B	Erectors, Boilermakers, Painters and Tender Shop
B.S.E	Engine Reception and Preparation
C	Concentration Yard
D1 and D2	Carpenters and Masons
E	Electrical Shop
F and F2	Smiths, Springsmiths and Chainmakers
G	Millwrights
H	Pattern Makers
J	Iron Foundry
J2	Chair Foundry
K	Coppersmiths and Sheet Metal Workers
L2	Tank Shop
M	Electric Sub-station
N	Bolt Shop
O	Tool Room
P1	Steaming and Boiler Mounting
P.L.	Loco Works, Platelayers, Rails, Roads and Water Mains Maintenance
Q	Angle Iron Smiths
R	Fitters, Turners and Machinemen
SP	Springsmiths
T	Brass Finishers
TH	Testing House
U	Brass Foundry
V	Boilermakers
W	Turners and Machinemen (Cylinder and Machine Shop)
X	Points and Crossings Fittings for Permanent Way
Z	Transport

The giant Erecting Shop, often described collectively as 'A' Shop, remained the principal feature of the sprawling works site. A vast edifice, it opened after 1901 and it was doubled after the Great War to cover nearly twelve acres. 'Undoubtedly one of the finest locomotive shops in the world' the GWR called it, and its principal purpose was to provide 'for progressive operations connected with locomotive erecting, fitting and wheeling'. It was really made up of four sections, which are labelled on

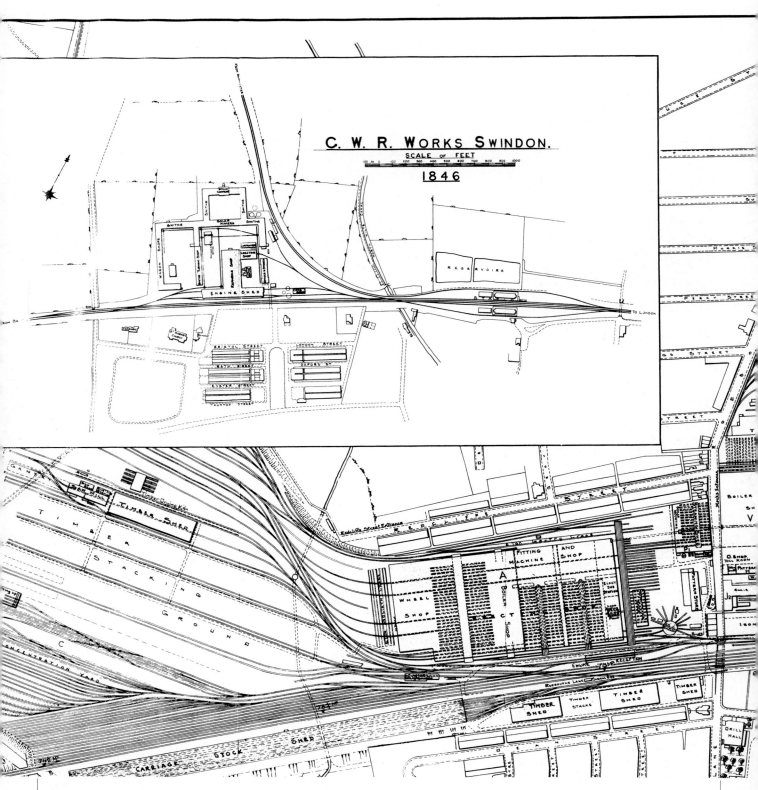

C. W. R. WORKS SWINDON.

SCALE OF FEET

1846

the plan. These were 'A' Erecting Shop, 'A' Machine and Fitting Shop, 'A' Boiler shop and 'A' Wheel Shop.

By 1948 the older part of the 'A' Erecting Shop had two electric traversers inside (with thirty-six roads running off each) and one outside, all for getting engines in and out, and round, the shops. The newer part of the building, opened in 1921, was that large part at the western end where the wheel shop was. This had a single traverser with sixty pits each a hundred feet long for dealing with the largest engines. The original part had four overhead cranes of 50 tons capacity and the newer one a further four overhead cranes, this time each capable of lifting 100 tons. This new portion held the famous Zeiss optical gear for aligning frames – a system later adopted at Doncaster. The celebrated engine testing plant was at the eastern end of the older part of the building, served by its own road off the outside traverser.

The stains and deposits of years out on the road had to be disposed off before work could begin and for

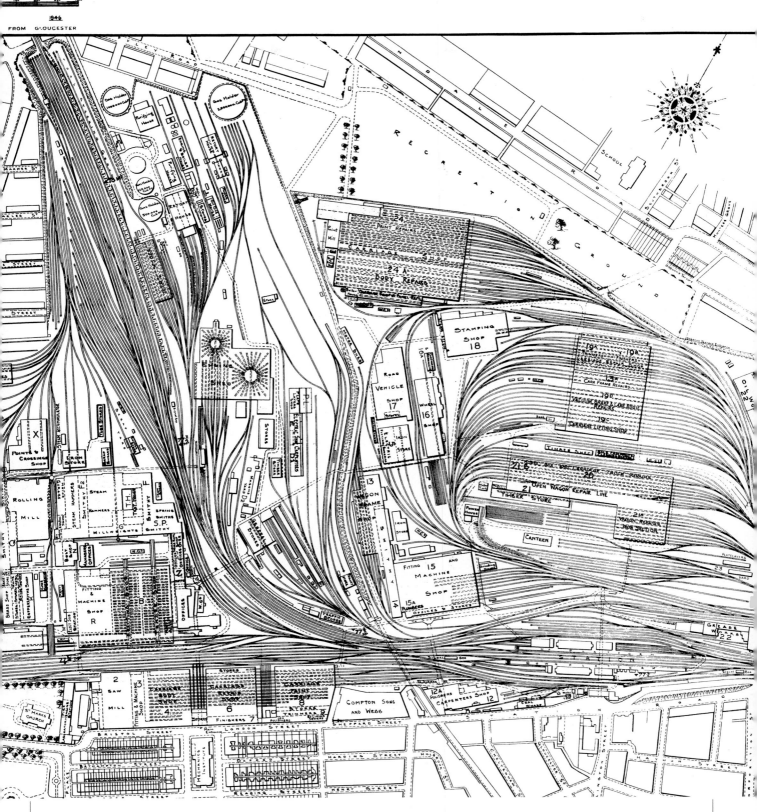

all the relatively advanced techniques at Swindon, the steam locomotive always needed plenty of old fashioned elbow grease. Consider the art of 'boshing': *'The cleaning or 'boshing' of locomotive parts is dealt with in systematic rotation in a plant situated in a central position within the main building. Trolleys are provided for conveying the parts stripped from the engine to the cleaning or 'boshing' plant. Each load is submerged in a boiling solution of sodium phosphate and is then raised and rinsed with cold water until clean. Approximately 180 tons of engine parts are boshed and inspected per week'.*

In the 'A' Machine and Fitting Shop all the motion, piston valves, rods and so on were repaired while the Boiler Shop was given up to the tumult and clamour of boiler, firebox and tank work. Men were injured and killed in a place like Swindon, hazards which were largely shrugged off as part of the job. Certainly little heed was given, either by management or men, to some of the more insidious dangers, such as

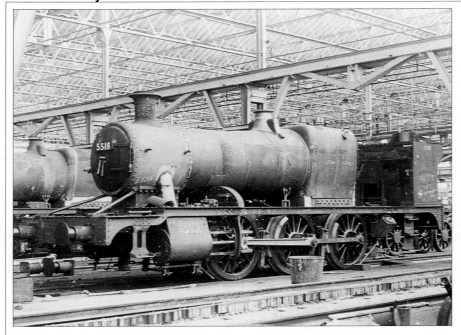

Top. A thoroughly unclothed 2-6-2T, No.5518, is being put back together – its wheels already painted – in 'A' Shop, 30 April 1950. Photograph H.C. Casserley.

Middle. 4-4-0 No.3382 under the vast 'A' Shop roof, 4 July 1947. Photograph H.C. Casserley.

Bottom. Even from the heights of the station roof the works seemed to go on for ever. This is the big C&W Machine Shop ('15' on the plan) in 1908. Though it had doors for fifteen roads, not all were used. The boarded crossing connects it with the station. This shop alone employed some 650 men, where fitters, turners and machinemen produced the fittings for vacuum brakes, axleboxes, drawgear, brakegear, steam heating apparatus and every wagon and coach accoutrement known to man. A faint line on the plan running across the front of the building represents in fact a set of narrow gauge rails, with tiny turntables at each end. A narrow gauge spur can just be seen on this print, just to the right and parallel to the boarded crossing at the far end. Outside the offices at the front, facing the main line, can just be seen one of the subways (not the famous one which led to the locomotive works and the shed) under the running lines.

noise. This was perhaps the least obvious of the threats and few riveters (or footplatemen for that matter) came to retirement without poor hearing. There is an extraordinary picture in one of the booklets, as late as 1947, in which a team of men tap the firebox stays of a firebox. While this is going on, two of the gang are *inside* the box! Quasimodo's experiences with the bells of Notre Dame could hardly have been worse…

The 'A' Wheel Shop dealt with something like 6,000 pairs of wheels a year. The processes involved bear repeating here: '*The operations involved in the preparation of a pair of locomotive driving wheels are many. The wheel centres are purchased as steel castings. The castings are first put into a large boring machine, which bores a hole in the boss for the axle. They are next marked off for the keyway, etc., then placed on a key-seating machine, which cuts the keyway. They are then taken to the hydraulic press, where the axle (supplied accurately machined by the machine shop) is placed in position for the wheels to be pressed on it. Suitable keys or wedges are then fitted and driven in. The wheels (now on the axle) are next placed in a turning lathe, which turns the rims for the tyres. After this the wheels are taken to a gas furnace where the tyres (already bored out) are heated and shrunk on, afterwards being firmly secured by a fastening which is rolled in place by machinery. The wheels are then placed in the lathe and tyres turned on the tread to*

You'll Remember those Black and White Days…

The diesel hydraulics meet the old order in the 1960s. Photograph I. Mackenzie, The Transport Treasury.

years machinery has figured largely in boiler construction, and the Swindon Boiler Shop is thoroughly and efficiently equipped in this direction. Worthy of notice is the large hydraulic flanging press which works at a pressure of 750 pounds to the square inch. The flanging of cold copper plates is carried out in this shop, which was the first to introduce that system. Boiler plates are cut out and edges shaped by the oxy-coal gas process, plate edge planing machine or guillotine shears. In addition to rolls, a vertical plate bending machine is installed. Drilling machines of the most up-to-date type are used and drilling jigs are employed wherever possible.'

Swindon, like all the great railway works, was self-contained and self-generating so far as was possible; at the far west of the site was the Concentration Yard ('C') designed to process all the myriad scrap which found its way to Swindon from all over the system. A purpose-built structure existed, equipped with overhead crane, cutters, shearing machines and lifting magnets. In the yard were three electric Goliath travelling cranes, from three to ten tons in capacity. These stacked and stored the scrap, loading it into wagons for taking away. Large castings were broken up with a drop ball from one of the Goliath cranes, in an area which had to be specially walled off to contain the flying pieces.

The Spring Shop ('SP') had been completely remodelled by 1948, with modern gas fired furnaces, their temperature controlled automatically. The entire Works had

the correct dimensions, after which they are put in a quartering machine which bores holes to receive the crank pins, which are pressed in the wheels by hydraulic press.'

In the Iron Foundry ('J') pig iron, scrap and coke were consumed, turned into molten iron to be served up from cupolas, at the rate of twelve tons of iron castings an hour each. Annual output was something like 10,000 tons, while a separate chair foundry produced a similar amount of tonnage of rail chairs, and other track parts. Probably the most complex casting was the combined cylinder and saddle for a King, and the biggest by 1948 was a 65 ton

anvil block for a four ton drop stamp.

The Brass Foundry ('U') brought forth some 1,700 tons of brass castings a year and in the Finishing Shop ('T') practically the whole of the brasswork that a locomotive needed was produced. An important part of the work was testing boiler mountings and gauges under live steam at up to 280lb pressure.

Next to the brass finishers was the Cylinder and Machine Shop ('W') where all the work of machining cylinders went on, together with certain operations to do with boiler foundation rings, smokebox doors and so on. Boilers were produced in the adjacent Boiler Shop ('V'): *'In later*

County No.1009 COUNTY OF CARMARTHEN with its 'tin' chimney and indicating apparatus for road testing on twenty coach trains, 7 November 1954. It was also tested on the Stationary Plant. Photograph P.J. Kelley.

'Finished' locos awaiting tenders were always a feature outside the shops; heading this row on 26 September 1959 were 7901 DODINGTON HALL and 6935 BROWSHOLME HALL. Photograph M.N. Bland, The Transport Treasury.

The End. With everything, so far as was humanly possible, conducted 'in house' Swindon of course, like many works, scrapped its own engines. It even did other Regions' condemned engines in the 1960s (V2s were being dealt with as late as 1964) though the sheer numbers involved meant that outside scrapyards did come to play a part. This is the Cutting Shed out on the western extremity where cranes and pits were provided for the purpose. It was a far cry from the private scrapyards where engines were crudely demolished in the open air. Ex-BP&GV 0-6-0T No.2165 (old No.12) approaches oblivion at the back while 2-6-2T No.4534 (both engines, it turns out were built in 1913 – the former by Hudswell Clarke, the 2-6-2T at Swindon) awaits the torch on 24 April 1955. The wheels in the foreground are the mortal remains of 2162, withdrawn a few weeks before. Photograph P.J. Kelley.

in fact benefited from a continuous series of improvements over the years, of which the GWR, gloomily contemplating nationalisation, was justly proud. Electric motors had replaced many steam engines and boilers; oxygen, acetylene and steam were widely piped around the shops and the gas works had been modernised. There was a boiler testing plant and a system of inspecting and testing purchased material had been instituted. The Research Department continued its work as never before. The internal system of transport was put under centralised control, resulting in considerable economy. Material, invariably heavy and bulky, was constantly on the move within the works and this was accomplished with a fleet of petrol trucks, with trailers. There was also a fleet of petrol-electric mobile cranes.

The Carriage and Wagon Department where the 'wooden engineers' held sway was a different world, generally both quieter, cooler and wholly less volcanic than the locomotive side of things. This is how the shops were arranged, as shown on the plan (numbers were not used in strict sequence, reflecting, presumably, changes over the years) *(see page 35).*The carriage works were, if anything, even more all-encompassing than the locomotive side, and it is not really *that* much of an exaggeration to say that rough sawn logs went in at one end and fully finished wagons and carriages came out at the other. Coarse logs were converted in the Sawmills into all the many basic parts necessary for carriage and wagon construction and repair. Drying kilns hastened the seasoning process. In the Carriage Body Shop coach bodies were built onto steel frames, and the specialised jobs were done in the Electrical Shop, Finishing Shop, Polishing Shop and so on. By 1948 of course much of the rest of the coach was of steel, though many wooden wagons still remained. Nearly 1,000 men were occupied in

wagon building and repair and latterly, come 1948, a new-style 'belt' system had been installed for the vast fleets of standard open wagons. Many of the shops in the C&W department bore little resemblance of course to the locomotive side of things. The Trimming Shop for instance looked more like a clothing factory, with men in white aprons cutting material with knives and rules on flat trimming tables. A peculiar institution was the Disinfecting Plant in which whole carriages were put into a sort of giant cylinder (housed inside a brick building of wholly conventional appearance) and treated with something noxious to kill vermin (fleas, in the main) and bacteria. The installation was also used to purify grain and flour wagons.

I hope this modest account based on the Great Western's own publicity material provides some sort of introduction at least to the vast enterprise that was Swindon Works, and manages to recall some part of its great splendour. Given its lingering demise and destruction, perhaps it's a useful time to remind ourselves of its bold and confident days at the very forefront of locomotive building and repair.

Thanks to Philip J. Kelley, Alec Swain and Eric Youldon in compiling this article.

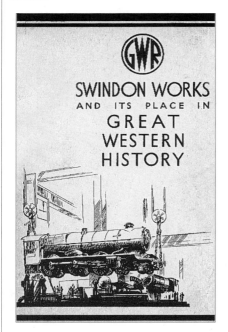

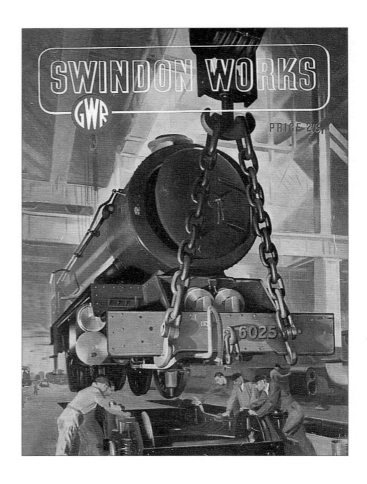

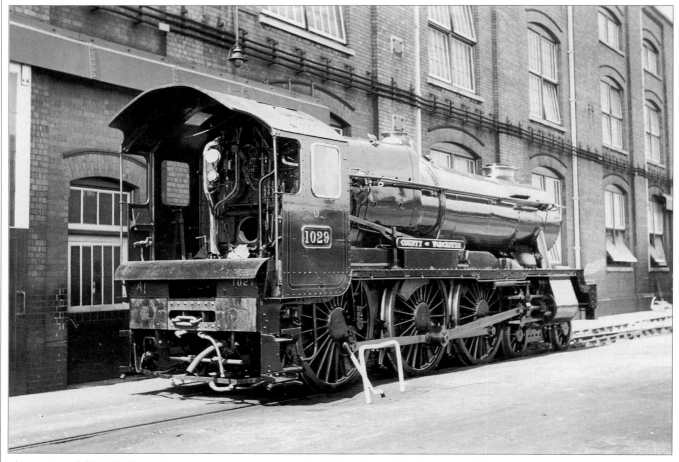

A pristine COUNTY OF WORCESTER. Photograph B. Richardson, The Transport Treasury.

You'll Remember those Black and White Days...

1	Sawmill (West End, by the Timber Stacking Ground)	
2	Sawmill	
3	Fitting and Machines	
4	Carriage Body Building	
5	Electric Train Lighting	
7A	Carriage Finishing	
7C	Polishers (Male)	
8	Carriage Painting	
9	Carriage Trimming	
9A	Lining Sewers (Female)	
10	Laundry (Female)	
10A	Polishers (Female)	
11	General Labourers	
12	Carpenters	
12A	Polishers	
13	Wagon Frame Building	
13A	Carriage Frame Repairs	
14	Smiths	
15	Fitting and Machines	
15A	Plumbers, Gas and Steam Fitters, Sheet Metal workers and Coppersmiths	
16	Wheels	
16A	Casehardening and Normalizing	
17	Road Vehicle Building and Repairing	
18	Stamping	
19A	Carriage Trippers Repairs	
19B	Carriage Finishers Repairs	
19C	Carriage Lifters	
19D	Vacuum Brake and Carriage Bogie Repairs	
20	Horse Box and Carriage Truck Repairs	
21	Wagon Building and Repairs, Wood Section	
21A	Wagon Repairs, Iron Section	
21B	Wagon Painting	
22	Oil and Grease Works	
23	Platelayers' Yard, Maintenance and Breaking-up Yard	
24	Carriage Paint Repairs	
24A	Carriage Body Repairs	

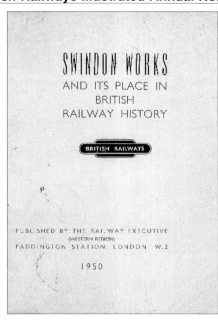

SWINDON WORKS
AND ITS PLACE IN
BRITISH
RAILWAY HISTORY

BRITISH RAILWAYS

PUBLISHED BY THE RAILWAY EXECUTIVE
(WESTERN REGION)
PADDINGTON STATION, LONDON, W.2

1950

Late in the day, in September 1964, 7924 THORNEYCROFT HALL undergoes overhaul. Signs of the times are an LM 2-6-0 on the right and, behind, one of the ill-fated D9500 hydraulics. Photograph Derek A. Potton, The Transport Treasury.

FOURUM MONTROSE SCORCHER

The summer of 1959 was a particularly glorious one and Montrose on the east coast of Scotland shared in the prolonged heatwave. V2 No.60965 of St Margarets shed (64A) passes Montrose North Box with the 3.40pm Aberdeen-Edinburgh Waverley express on 4 July 1959. The train had taken the former North British route at Kinnaber Junction before skirting the shore of Montrose Basin. Ahead lay Arbroath, Dundee and the Tay and Forth bridges.

Aberdeen (61B) based V2 No.60835, in charge of the 12.30pm from Aberdeen to Edinburgh Waverley, runs through Montrose on 8 August 1964. Despite its grimy condition and imminent demise, the engine still managed to look rather fine in the bright sunshine. The tide is out in Montrose Basin and the skyline is blurred by a shimmering heat haze.

In blistering heat, B1 No.61146 of Thornton (62A) arrives at Montrose on 4 July 1959 with the 12.40pm from Glasgow Buchanan Street. The rambling brick and timber Arbroath & Montrose Railway buildings provided ample if undistinguished accommodation. Some of the villas of this attractive town can be seen above the train.

Kinnaber Junction was one of the most celebrated places on the entire British railway network because of its role in the Races to Aberdeen. On 8 August 1964, V2 No.60973 of Dundee shed (62B), leaves the East Coast main line with the 11.00am summer Saturday Glasgow Buchanan Street-Aberdeen working. The train ran via Dundee rather than using the West Coast Strathmore line on the right. Photos and notes by W.A.C. Smith, captions by Paul Anderson.

A While Longer

A recent *Fourum*, in BRILL Vol.10 No.1, enabled us to share in J.G. Walmsley's visit to the charming little engine shed at Three Bridges in Sussex, on 11 May 1963; the temptation to revisit it here, with further photographs, proved irresistible. The shed's demise (though it lasted for some years in use for stock purposes and was still a sort of 'time capsule' in the 1970s) was not far off. By May 1963 whole areas of the country had seen the complete demise of steam and main line steam everywhere was in headlong retreat, yet Three Bridges contrived to retain an almost pre-Group atmosphere. Here, H tank 31518 takes coal in time-honoured fashion – this strange walkway was erected to assist coaling but it was not high enough – hence the somewhat hairy position taken up by the coalman, guiding the coal box with a borrowed shunter's pole. Photograph J.G. Walmsley, The Transport Treasury.

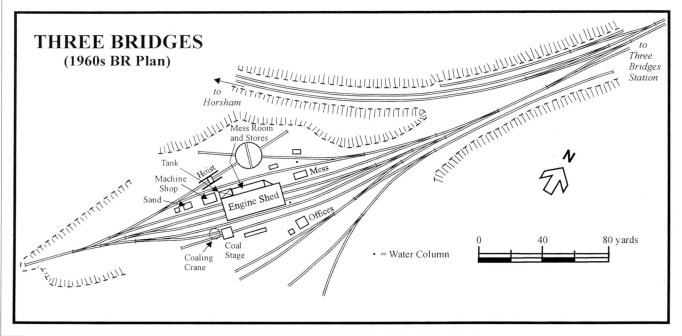

THREE BRIDGES
(1960s BR Plan)

to Horsham

Mess Room and Stores

Tank

Hoist

Machine Shop

Sand

Mess

Engine Shed

Offices

Coal Stage

Coaling Crane

to Three Bridges Station

N

• = Water Column

0   40   80 yards

t Three Bridges

0-6-0s and 0-4-4Ts characterised Three Bridges probably like no other shed in the land by this late date. 30545 and 30546 sit about the yard – signs of the times are D6500 lurking in the background and the appalling quality of the coal, a mix of pressed cobbles and dust. Photographs J.G. Walmsley, The Transport Treasury.

H 0-4-4T 31518, a refugee from Kent, was often to be found at Three Bridges at this time. It carries a Tunbridge Wells West (75F) shedplate and would be lucky to survive the closure of its home shed later in the year, in September 1963. By about this time Three Bridges was also using ex-LSW 0-4-4Ts on its East Grinstead push-pull jobs; on 16 June 1963 for instance, *The Railway Observer* reported M7 30015 sharing the turn with H 31263. Both of course were 'foreign' to this ex-LBSC shed. Two more M7s were on shed, 30133 under repair and 30029 dead, and there were still two withdrawn K class moguls stored in the yard at the time. Photograph J.G. Walmsley, The Transport Treasury.

The shed was in fact very modern in its layout and engines could turn and coal and run round to whichever end of the shed was easiest for the next job, with minimal interruption or fuss. H class tank 31518 is at the end of its servicing routine, steam up, bunker piled high and pointing the right way for its next task. Photograph J.G. Walmsley, The Transport Treasury.

31518 on the ash road, 11 May 1963. It was dead on the shed by June the following year, 1964, and did not finally leave for cutting up at Norwich until September. Photograph J.G. Walmsley, The Transport Treasury.

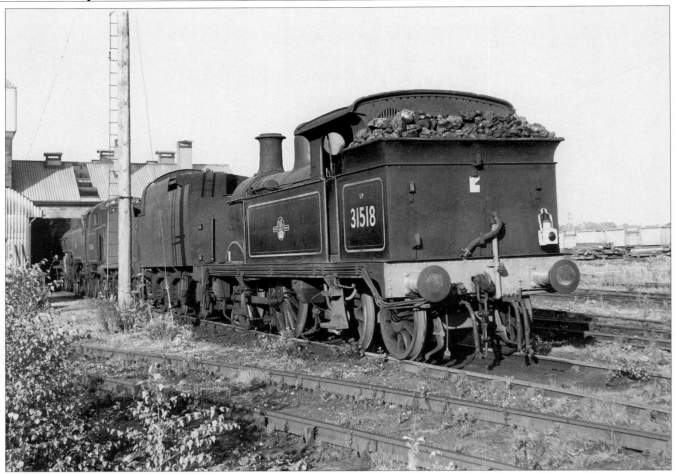

J.G. Walmsley was not the only visitor to this rustic idyll. Alec Swain went there on 15 September 1963 and photographed – what else – 31518 in excellent nick with a half-decent bunker of coal. Three Bridges was by now a staging post for withdrawn locos on their way to various breakers. The two tenders behind 31518 (one off a Q1) are indications of gathering dereliction while the BR 2-6-4T might well be 80084, reported stored around this time. Photograph Alec Swain, The Transport Treasury.

And Peter Groom too! These are the two stored K 2-6-0s already mentioned, 32345 and 32353, on 22 April 1963. Photograph Peter Groom.

Another Tunbridge Wells West H class tank, 31005, visits the hoist for attention on 15 September 1963. The garden shed-style covers either side, to provide shelter for the fitters, were thoroughly home-made – and typical of this delightful little shed. Models of it should be appearing on layouts across the land! Photograph Alec Swain, The Transport Treasury.

Snow Hill

Haunting Snow Hill and capturing its *ancien régime* atmosphere, Michael Mensing caught all the comings and goings of the wonderful, doomed, station. Typical of the times was the steam-diesel changeover; on 1 April 1961 for instance, 2-6-2T 4104 stood with the 5.45pm to Dudley and Brettell Lane while one of the new DMU local sets waited with the 4.25pm Wellington-Lapworth.

D827 KELLY makes a fine sight in the shadow with the 7.30am Shrewsbury-Paddington on 13 October 1962.

Interiors

Tucked away over on Platform 12, with its own shed-like exhaust hood, 6935 BROWSHOLME HALL quietly waits with the 5.45pm to Worcester Shrub Hill via Stratford on Avon, on 16 April 1960.

Wonderful scene on 17 June 1957, as 1022 COUNTY OF NORTHAMPTON arrives with the Birkenhead-Bournemouth. 9614 is light engine; one of the delights of Snow Hill was to see one of these tanks scurry through when the great station was more or less empty. All photographs Michael Mensing

A ROYAL SOVEREIGN

Languishing out of use with internal damage, having broken its inside connecting rod on its home GE Section, 2871 MANCHESTER CITY was chosen in 1944 as the first B17 to be rebuilt to the new standard two cylinder B2. It finally emerged from Darlington Works in August 1945. It had only got the MANCHESTER CITY plates back in 1937 because the real owner, 2870, was forced to become TOTTENHAM HOTSPUR (did the authorities have *no* conception of how mortifying this could be?). In February 1946, as a new B2, 2871 got the new number 1671 and was selected for royal work, MANCHESTER CITY giving way to ROYAL SOVEREIGN a few months later. It was now the official royal engine, pride of Cambridge shed. Its regular work outside of royal duties was Liverpool Street in the morning and Kings Cross and back in the afternoon. In these two photographs, 61671 is at Cambridge with the 3.10pm buffet express to Kings Cross, on 17 May 1952 (above) and below – in typical sparkling condition – on 24 February 1953.

You'll Remember those Black and White Days...

There was another twist to the story, for the ROYAL SOVEREIGN shown here was withdrawn in 1958 and in October of that year the name passed to 61632 (formerly BELVOIR CASTLE). On this page 61671 is at Cambridge again on the buffet express job. Above, ex-works after a year on the 3.25pm Kings Cross buffet on 3 June 1950 and below with Driver Hudson preparing to leave with the 3.10pm buffet, 20 May 1953. All photographs M.N. Bland, The Transport Treasury.

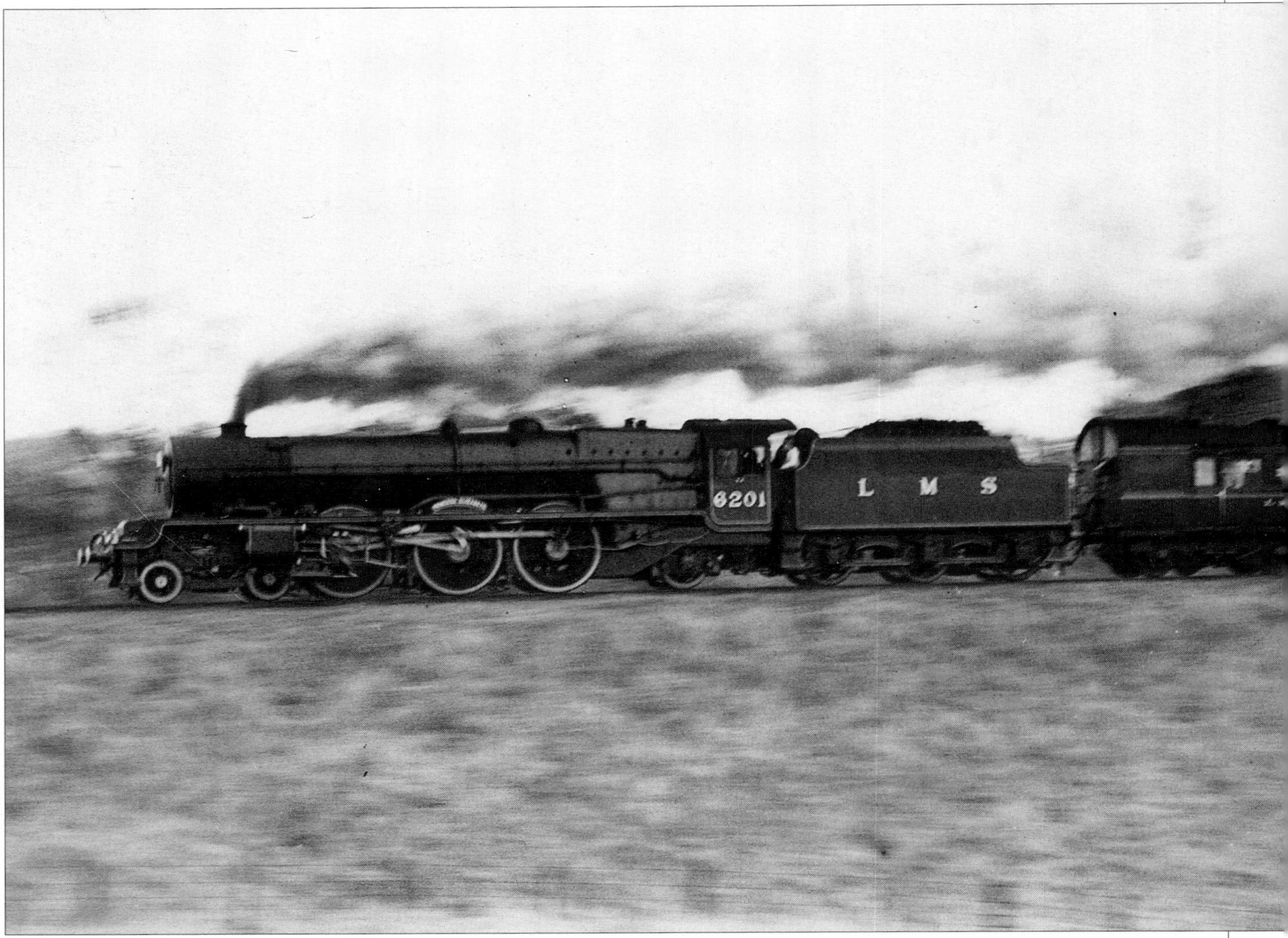
6201
L M S

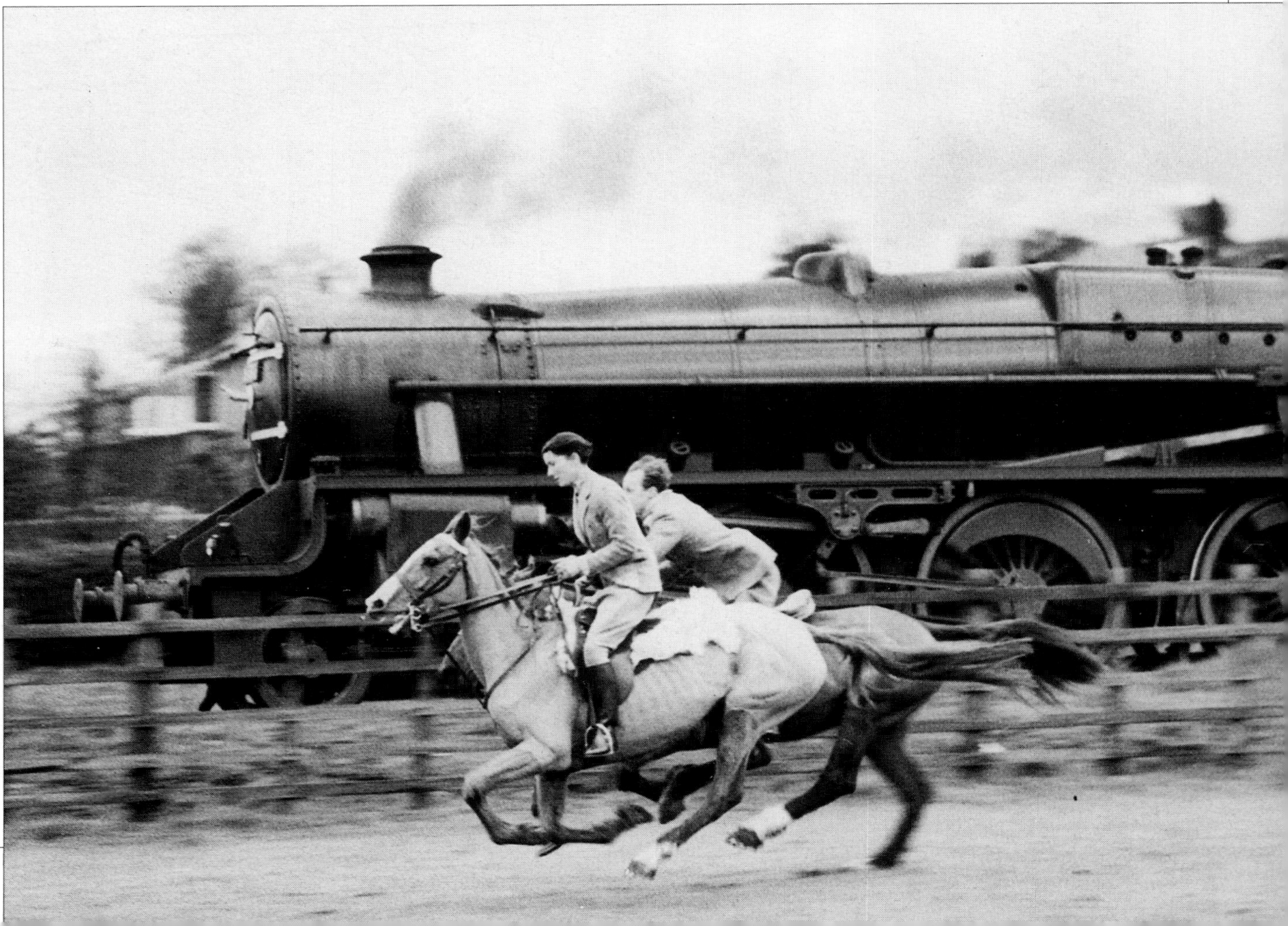

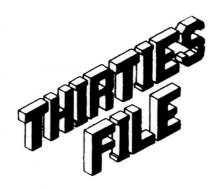

LMS Racers

A Princess Royal Pacific in its pomp, 6201 PRINCESS ELIZABETH on its record-breaking run of 16 November 1935, when the 401½ miles from Euston to Glasgow were covered in under six hours. Brian Haresnape in his book *Stanier Locomotives* (Ian Allan) identifies the boffin in the white coat as R.A. Riddles, destined to become the grand old man of BR steam.

A wonderful publicity photograph taken for the LMS in the 1930s. 5181 was one of a large batch from Armstrong Whitworth in 1935, so it is probably a safe bet that this is the year in question, or perhaps 1936. The context in which this carefully obtained photograph was used (if at all) is now long lost to us though the imagery of speed, pedigree and so on is obvious. What, though, might the private thoughts of the driver be, we can wonder...

NEW SIGNAL BOX AT STAFFORD

Looking north from the platform ends in April 1953 with the new No.5 box on the left. The old No.5 opposite has gone. To the left of the new box is the far extremity of Stafford shed yard, with the top of a loco just visible. On the right a 2P (this would be one of the two used as station pilots in this period – 40443 or 40461) shunts a pair of vans – the total capacity of that headshunt! The Bagnall Locomotive works is on the left behind the new box, on the other side of the road; the bridge, accordingly, was 'Bagnall's Bridge'.

In early 1953 colour light signals and an improved track layout came into use at Stafford on the West Coast main line and a new No.5 signalbox built for the new arrangements. This was erected opposite the existing No.5, which was then taken out of use. The new box controlled the up and down fast and slow lines at the north end of the station, and the junctions with the lines to Wellington and Stafford Common. The new box and combined relay was in the familiar style of the time (Euston, among many others) and though demonstrably ugly, the authorities were very proud of it: *it has been constructed in accordance with agreed modern standards with brick walls faced with hand made bricks, reinforced concrete roof and wide vision metal windows. The building is centrally heated by a thermostatically controlled gas fire boiler and is equipped with modern electric lighting.'*

The 123 levers in the old box had become uneconomical to maintain, and could not have been altered to operate the remodelled permanent way. The operating floor of the old box was 23 feet above rail level, largely to give the signalman a view of the line to the north of an adjoining bridge. This, however, meant he could not readily see trains passing the signalbox during bad visibility. The operating floor of the new signalbox was only 12ft 6ins above ground level, but the provision of track circuits and the latest electrical controls, it was considered, would more than compensate for any loss of visibility during clear weather.

Because Stafford was such an important junction, colour light running signals were installed on the main lines controlled by the new No.5 box; these formed the first part of a complete multiple aspect colour light signalling system which was intended to improve traffic working through Stafford generally. Such a system included the modern safeguard of continuous track circuiting, and greatly improved the working of trains during bad visibility.

The new mechanical lever frame was of the normal LMR pattern with catch handle locking and had 150 levers. All the points and so on were mechanically operated, along with the ground signals provided for shunting purposes.

You'll Remember those Black and White Days...

April 1953, and a view south from 'Bagnall's Bridge' with the new box on the right; beyond, the coaling plant of the engine shed rears up.

From 'Bagnall's Bridge', looking north towards Crewe, April 1953. The line to Wellington goes off to the left, Crewe straight ahead and the old Great Northern line through Stafford Common to the right. From left to right the lines here are Down Slow, Up Slow, Down Fast and Up Fast.

FOURUM Changes in the Life of GLASGOW HIGHLANDER

You'll Remember those Black and White Days...

45157 GLASGOW HIGHLANDER at Balornock (St Rollox) shed in May 1948, in very early BR livery. The 31A shedplate (NOT Cambridge!) heralds the LMS system of shed coding which would soon be imposed on BR. Note the high position of the cabside number – so that it was not obscured by the retracted tablet catcher. Power classification is simply '5'. She looks to be 'bulled-up' for some reason and is almost certainly ex-works; the cylinder and piston valve end covers are highly polished, and there is evidence of cotton waste on the footplate just ahead of the cab.

45157 takes water at Balquhidder on 23 May 1955, with the 12.12pm Glasgow-Oban. She now carries a 65B (St Rollox by now, under Eastfield) shedplate. One might think the train warranted more than a 'stopping passenger' headcode (the lamp itself is slightly 'at sea') but perhaps this reflects local practice – see next photograph for instance. There is just a trace of the tablet catcher and the cabside number is now in the standard position, albeit in the larger ScR numerals.

45157 with first BR emblem pilots another named Black Five, 45158 GLASGOW YEOMANRY on the 9.18am Oban-Glasgow, passing Crianlarich Junction on 5 May 1956, with just three coaches – perhaps it represents a 'balancing' working, like the Black Five with CITY OF LONDON elsewhere in this Annual. Another Black Five with five coaches has got the road to leave.

45157 in later days at Stirling, with later BR emblem and fitted with BR AWS and cover missing off the top feed – times have changed. The boiler cladding is a little adrift too, just behind the top feed, just as it was in the previous photograph! All photographs J.L. Stevenson; notes by Alec Swain.

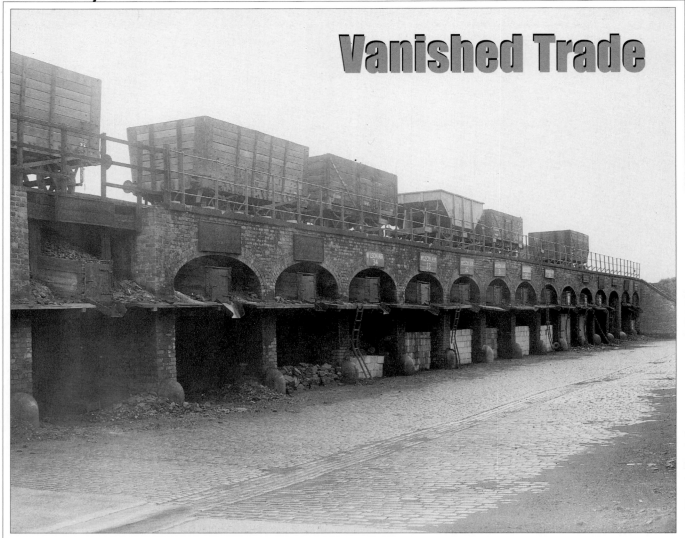

Vanished Trade

When we lament the passing of the coal trade on our railways we are really lamenting only a much simplified and attenuated version of the great, vast business upon which the railways first built their wealth and power. We remember endless bouncing four wheel wagons, trundling along hypnotically behind 9Fs, WDs, 8Fs and all the rest but forget that, before all that coal could be delivered at last to its customers, wholly more intricate arrangements had to be made. The fatal flaw in the business was that, in the end, so much of it was reduced to single or a few wagonloads and these became steadily less economically viable with every year that went by. BR became exasperated in the end and was finally thwarted in its desire to raise the main body of its coal trade above the level of the single wagonload. Block loads did come of course, but much lesser business had to be abandoned along the way.

There were few works prepared to go to the expense of enlarging their handling apparatus and even the biggest in the land – the exporting staithes and giant cranes to be found in the North East and in South Wales

for instance, continued to process the humble four wheel wagon. It was not just the customers of course, for the transition would cost BR hundreds of millions of pounds (the massive fleet of loose coupled mineral wagons would have to be vacuum fitted for instance) before it got any return; such a process would take years, and was anyway guaranteed eventually to be curtailed as the government of the day felt the next economic pinch. Another problem was that, even if the big customers could somehow be convinced or cajoled, there was no hope for the myriad local sites such as these – and how could the railway continue to run both systems?

In a way, the local coal trade to individual customers was doomed even before the 1940s were beginning to come to an end. The Leeman Road drops at York, pictured in July 1956, perfectly illustrate the problem – as well as the local variation which characterised the North East, the use of bottom doors rather than side or end doors found everywhere else. That was another thing! The North East had coal drops instead of the sleeper-built coal pens found in other parts of the country

but the principle was the same; individual wagons would arrive off the trip goods to be unloaded and distributed according to individual customer, and there could be several coal merchant customers in any one yard. It was the 'coal concentration schemes of the 1950s and 1960s which sought to eradicate these wasteful movements. One huge problem was the sheer amount of time the coal spent in BR's wagons; BR was effectively picking up the bill for warehousing the stuff for weeks on end. Another problem was that all the local yards were very old and run-down; they needed improvements for which there was no money and it was more difficult every year to find the staff to man them. Observe how ancient these drops are – the wooden chutes are creaking with age, the timber platforms groaning with the weight of years and the brickwork increasingly battered. The ladders are almost unusable, bent by years of lorries backing into them. It's impossible of course to describe the decline of coal on BR in a little over 500 words – only to hint at some of the reasons. Maybe these pictures are more eloquent demonstration!

CENTREPIECE
High summer at Kings Cross

In what passes for high summer at Kings Cross, that is, oven heat, haze, throat-grasping air and thunderous noise, George Heiron photographs two of the best that the place could offer: ALCAZAR and GOLDEN FLEECE, in August 1958. *(George Heiron has a book in preparation for Ian Allan, devoted to his photographs and his much sought-after paintings – watch out for it!)*

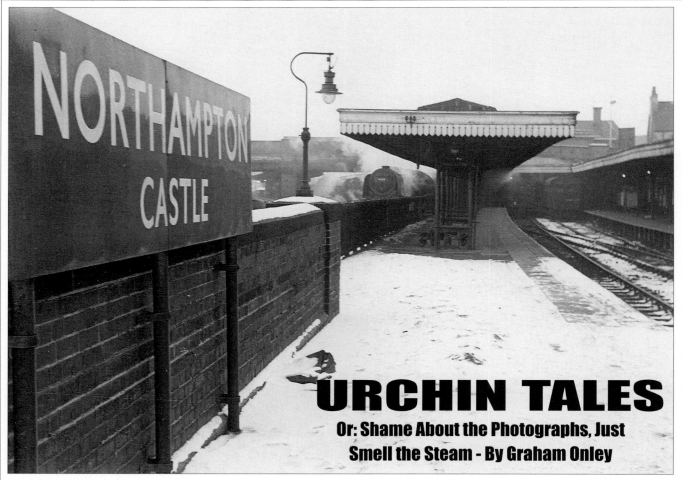

URCHIN TALES

Or: Shame About the Photographs, Just
Smell the Steam - By Graham Onley

The freezing platforms, 46248 safely settled in. The oiks have scarpered to the platform ends to await its departure. Photograph Graham Onley.

Had the viciously cold, foggy and snow-laden winter of 1962-63 arrived a couple of years or so earlier, a good many intrepid enthusiasts may not have considered forsaking the weekend fireside for photographic purposes. Had they considered anything during that Arctic winter, it would probably have revolved around stoking up the coal fire, watching the wrestling on the telly (remember that?) and waiting for *Sports Report* on the Light Programme to hear just which sports fixtures had managed to survive the weather.

On 2nd February 1963 there was little soccer or other sport played due to the weather conditions, and as wrestling was very much a minority interest to most of our squad, the majority decision was to assemble at Northampton Castle station *just* to see (hopefully) a steam hauled 'Carlisle stopper'. Such a decision was not totally surprising even allowing for the freezing daytime temperature. To be honest, the forecast of more snow actually tempted one or two of us outdoors to see if we could emulate some of the snow shots seen in railway magazines in previous years.

The joint decision made, push bikes deposited outside the station entrance (and still there one and

three quarter hours later), 2d Platform Tickets duly purchased, our way made over the footbridge and we were standing expectantly at the north end of Platform 6, cameras at the ready, a few minutes before the appointed time. The appointed time came and went; the 'Carlisle stopper' did not. We were not perturbed. Trains did not only run late because of the heavy weather, and delay meant that the likelihood of the train actually being steam hauled increased. The chance of such an outcome, it seemed, was in direct proportion to the increasing lateness.

Almost thirty five years later, I cannot pinpoint the exact amount of lateness. At that period of my life I had little interest in recording passing times and numbers of coaches/wagons on passing trains. Now I thank those who did for their foresight, wishing I had been a little (or even a lot) sharper! I suppose it must have been about 3.30pm when the peg for the up fast turn-in to the main platform 1 was pulled off by the signalman in Northampton number 2 box.

Our prayers were well and truly answered, reward for being outdoors on such a foul afternoon coming in the form of Coronation Pacific 46248 CITY OF LEEDS which coasted in and halted at the platform, about

thirty minutes behind schedule. By this time 8F 2-8-0 48676 had been patiently waiting at the up through road peg for at least 45 minutes. Obviously it was not going to be turned out onto the long stiff climb to Roade, via the direct line, in front of the express. With the benefit of hindsight, I suppose that with the late running of the express, 48676 and its heavy coal train could have been well away, south of Roade, (where 46248 would have been turned onto the main line again) before the Pacific would have been within striking distance. I still wonder why it was not sent out much sooner, as the express more often than not took the longer route via Blisworth. What might have been happening in the mysterious 'Control' with the all-seeing eyesight its inhabitants were endowed with?

Despite the main attraction, the somewhat unusual sight of a Cricklewood 2-8-0 on our patch did not escape notice. We were however astonished to see that 48676 still carried an early version of BR front number plate, complete with serifed numbers. I suppose many of this style did in reality survive until ultimate withdrawal of their bearers, but we did not see many. Sightings of such non-standard mundanities were restricted to the 'closed' 6 on occasional Stanier 2-6-0s and certain Class 5 4-6-0s. Over later years I have seen photographic proof that we neither saw nor knew everything, and it is this continuing fascinating state of discovery that I find, well, fascinating. A question often considered at camp fire discussions was (and still is) the absence of front number plates on all ex-LNWR locos entering BR ownership. Does anyone know please?

Even now there may still be questions raised as to the point of turning out in such weather, but there were valid reasons driving us ever onwards. The need to photograph as much of the (by now rapidly accelerating) passing scene will be remembered by many readers. Those of our squad who could manage membership of the local branch of the RCTS by virtue of the massive wages and salaries then being earned, sometimes approaching £10 a week, often became the bearers of bad news, courtesy of the wonderful *Railway Observer*, published monthly, then as now, by that august organisation. The current, by that date seemingly always, bad news was to be found in the January 1963 edition of the 'RO'. A look in the general British Railways section revealed that among the large number of steam locos stored were almost countless Jubilees, Patriots, Scots, Princess Royals and even *Duchesses*, as well as similarly large

numbers of top link locos from other regions less near to home. Many of were already withdrawn, and it was confidently (but very sadly) forecast that few would return to steam before their inevitable withdrawal. The same issue recorded the extinction of the Princess Royals, unrebuilt Patriots and the lone 71000 – but part of the highest number of express loco withdrawals yet seen in one fell swoop. The same story was repeated for all other regions.

Was it any surprise that the possibility of a Duchess on the Carlisle stopper outweighed the urge to stay by the fireside, and how right we were to be proved a few days later, when sight of the pale green-covered February edition of the 'RO' produced further bad news which was almost more than could be borne. The last month of 1962 had, as half expected, produced unprecedented destruction of all types, sizes and parentage of loco. The London Midland and the Scottish regions withdrew countless members of the old LMS express classes. So did the Eastern and the North Eastern regions where they had been lucky enough to inherit some of our ex-LMS locos. Their actions, we considered, were the ultimate in bad taste. Mass entry to the first available monastery was narrowly averted thanks to the table-topping position of Northampton Town in the old Division Three.

While 46248 simmered fairly patiently at the platform, had it not

been so cold, our thoughts would probably have drifted back a little to the days prior to the first week of 1960, when our friend the 'Carlisle Stopper' took the main line, calling at Blisworth at about the same time that it now called at Northampton Castle. The connecting train in this instance ran from Northampton to Blisworth at 2.32pm. It was the habit, if such is the right description for a relatively infrequent event, of those of us who travelled on this train behind one of our local twins, Ivatt Class 2 2-6-2Ts 41218 or 41219, to wait on the platform at Blisworth to watch the arrival and departure of the 'stopper'. This gave us an opportunity to actually see a Duchess moving slowing enough for us to savour the sight. To watch and hear the locomotive getting its train away again was, to use a modern description, awesome. We would probably have described it as 'great'.

My personal acquaintance with the train during its Blisworth days was really for no more than seven or eight years, and then infrequently. The loss felt by the January 1960 closure of Blisworth station to passengers was, to my young feelings, a blow much softened by the anticipation of another daytime express being diverted permanently to pass our own stamping ground. During its Blisworth days, motive power was often a Duchess, but I had managed to see Rebuilt Scots, Patriots of both types, even piloted

The unfortunate 48676 waits alongside the Pacific. Photograph Graham Onley.

Jubilees, and the occasional Britannia, including Polmadie's 70050 FIRTH OF CLYDE on one memorable occasion.

My own highlight was that of a Duchess piloted by an LMS 2P 4-4-0 during either 1957 or 1958. In those days it was believed that a regulation existed to the effect that Stanier Pacifics were not to be double-headed. This was hardly surprising to us as we could not conceive of any size of train that could possible be beyond the ability of one of these favourites. For years afterwards I felt that I had seen something illicit, something to keep quiet about, but then various photographs were published showing more than one Duchess double-headed combin-ation so I began to feel a little more comfortable with the memory! I admit however that the sound of that piloted Duchess slithering and sliding away from Blisworth with what was a fairly heavy train is nicely tucked away into said memory bank. The accompanying sight, viewed from the canal bridge south of the station, 200 yards across the fields on the down

On its way, with the Fireman leaning in for a shovelfull. Photograph Graham Onley.

side of the line is never to be forgotten.

Getting back to the present, or rather the more recent past, I had decided that with the highly imminent withdrawal of so many of our old friends, there was work to be done. Therefore as 46248 pulled away from the platform I took to the bay platforms from where I was able to take a number of what I considered to be unusual shots of

various parts of the loco, such as the broadside front end, the midships, and the cabside before settling for a final shot of CITY OF LEEDS passing a northbound Class 5 on a fitted freight. Having waited for over an hour, our reward was to be a steam-wreathed going away shot of 48676 as it set sail chasing 46248. I don't suppose it ever caught up!

Ye Grate Beeste moves off into the murk, as a Class Five arrives on a fitted freight. Photograph Graham Onley.

DIESEL DAWN Ugly Ducklings

Once it became a mechanism to spread the business round as many parliamentary constituencies as possible, rather than produce a good, standard, reliable fleet, the Modernisation Plan threw up some strange beasts. Their looks suffered further as the builders, often unused to the new form of power, continued to construct an engine and a body outline (even the bunker in this class!) around a nominal traditional 0-6-0T. The apotheosis of this was probably the 204hp Hudswell Clarke series, with their steam locomotive chimneys (presumably just taken from stock at the works!) for the exhaust. D2500-2509 (original numbers 11116-11120, 11144-11148) had come from the builders in 1956 and were all at Birkenhead shed for dock working. The class disappeared with the liquidation of the non-standard shunting fleet and all went in 1967. In this photograph, D2509 stands at its home shed Birkenhead, with the ash tower in the background and thoroughly disreputable-looking 'jocko – a 3F tank – alongside. Photograph The Transport Treasury.

11700 of the 1953-56 series of NB 200hp shunters went to West Hartlepool shed in 1953 and was there for years with the next two. It has many exterior differences from say, 11705 top overleaf and is very appropriately shown in its customary state – out of use with coupling rods on the footplate – probably at West Hartlepool. Becoming D2700, it was the first of the eight locos to go out of service, by two or three years, in 1963. Photograph The Transport Treasury.

Scotland, for some reason, seemed to get more than its fair share of the 'ugly ducklings' than other Regions. The little North British 200hp diesel hydraulic 0-4-0s originally numbered 11700-11707 (later D2700-2707) came out from 1953 to 1956, altering in shape over that time. 11705 found a natural home at Edinburgh St Margarets, where odd little tanks had long made a living from the various shunts around the city. The remains of the roundhouse where their steam predecessors had stabled (and continued to stable) made a suitable home for the diesels in their turn. 11705 (with 11704 on one of the old roundhouse stalls beyond, and a steam locomotive just out of sight to the right) was on the little turntable on 7 July 1957, having suffered a small dent on its cabside. They did not work well, were overcomplicated things in a thoroughly steam environment and bounced and jinked alarmingly as they travelled out to their jobs. All had gone by early 1968. Photograph The Transport Treasury.

Amongst the ugliest of the ugly ducklings were the offerings of Barclay; 11180 (it became D2403) was built in 1956 and was not finally withdrawn until January 1969. it went new to Lincoln in October 1956 but was at Immingham after that. This is where it is in this picture, early in its career before the 'wasp' black and yellow stripes were added. The ridiculous 'hump' was the fuel tank which, apart from largely nullifying the visual advantages of the cab (so useful on a shunting engine) held 400 gallons of fuel oil on the 0-6-0s and 325 gallons on the 0-4-0s. Photograph The Transport Treasury.

You'll Remember those Black and White Days...

One of the smaller Barclay shunters, the first of what became, a bit optimistically, BR Class 01. Four of them were introduced in 1956, 11503-11506 and two later ended up on the Holyhead Breakwater. The ladder, provided on the left-hand side only, was for a man to clamber up with a fuel line. 11503 became D2953 and was withdrawn in 1966. All four were stationed at Stratford for shunting restricted sites; 11503 was photographed there on 28 September 1956, a few months after going into traffic. Photograph The Transport Treasury.

Just to demonstrate that not only the BR Modernisation Scheme spawned ugly ducklings... The Southern too could come up with a brute and, complete with 'Bulleid' wheels, 500hp 0-6-0 No.11001 appeared out of Ashford works in 1950. The most powerful shunter to work on BR, the intention was to use it on trip work as well as shunting. For this it arrived at Norwood Junction in May 1950. Later in the year it was working from Feltham on 'hump' shunting and local trip work but after this it seems to have settled down at Norwood Junction; it was photographed there in the shed yard in September 1957, a few weeks after withdrawal. Photograph Tony Wright.

Station Survey
A Tale of Two Welwyns

Separated by three quarters of a century, it could hardly be expected that the two Welwyns should be closely akin in their style and looks. Welwyn (the 'North' came a little later, after Welwyn Garden City opened; it shows on LNER plans of 1938 for instance) was a homely little place, a station on the main line but indisputably still a by-way. Here it is at the end of 1963, 6 December, with everyone praying that the winter would not be like the one before! Note the London Transport bus stop just visible behind the tree on the right, by the bus shelter. Oh for the days of the Green rover ticket...

The somewhat pioneering and now long-lamented journal *Locomotive News and Railway Notes* published a series in 1921 entitled *The Highways and By-Ways of a Great Railway*. This described, in a detail which was then not customary in railway matters, the main line of the Great Northern north from Kings Cross into the unknown hinterlands of Hertfordshire, Bedfordshire and Huntingdonshire. These places were,

in truth, another country then. Welwyn was famous for its magnificent viaduct and not much else, though the countryside was considered amongst the prettiest in the land: *'Many regular travellers affirm that the landscape view which is obtainable from the summit of these lofty brick arches is the finest on the GN main line, or even on the whole East Coast route to Edinburgh. We see a charmingly wooded valley far*

below, with a stream flowing peacefully along, and obtain a wide outlook over undulating, leafy, typical English country.' As pleasant a place as it may be still, the area is hardly likely to attract the same comment today.

There was only one Welwyn station then, and it was barely noticed by R.A.H. Weight (the correspondent of *The Locomotive News and Railway Notes*) as he sped

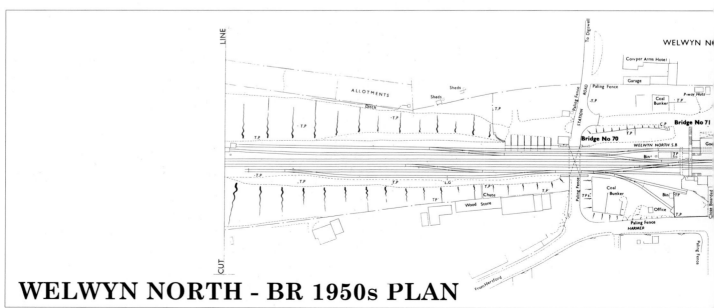

WELWYN NORTH - BR 1950s PLAN

north though, blessed with far sight, he more or less predicted the coming of the second station. First the first, so to speak. Welwyn station appears to have opened with the main line in 1850, and Wrottesley (*The Great Northern Railway Volume One*, Batsford, 1979) records the scene on 5 August that year, with the inspection train stopping at Welwyn for the party to descend into the pretty valley of the little River Mimram, to admire 'the splendid viaduct'. This was a Monday, and public opening of the line took place two days later. The station does not appear to have changed all that much throughout its life and it is still clearly recognisable today.

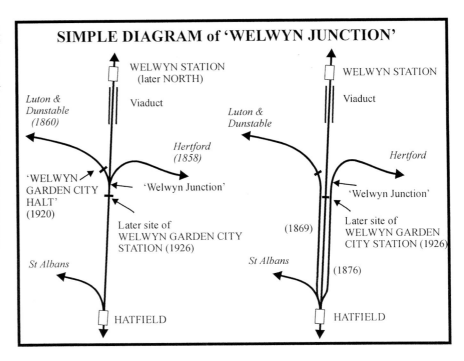

SIMPLE DIAGRAM of 'WELWYN JUNCTION'

The up side buildings, 6 December 1963, still with the gas lamps so familiar from the GN line stations at that time. The little crossing and its simple wooden steps was there for the staff, but they would need to be nerveless daredevils today, such is the frequency, speed and relative silence of the electric trains. The prospects of electrification had in fact surfaced now and then over the years but it was still a good few years off – the publicity poster has to rely on the work then going on between Crewe and Liverpool/Manchester. Better than that, Elvis was on at the Embassy, in G.I. Blues.

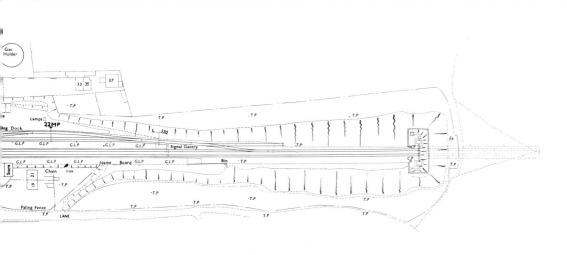

Looking north to the 446 yard South Welwyn tunnel, 6 December 1963. (The GN labelled this tunnel so and the next one north was North Welwyn; in later days the names seem to have been reversed to Welwyn South and Welwyn North.) Both platforms have now been lengthened towards the tunnel portal, to accommodate eight car trains. The loading dock on the left has high and low portions, for high and low sided wagons – there was no subtlety that was beyond the Great Northern!

The view south from the portal above South Welwyn (or Welwyn South) tunnel, 30 March 1943, straight as an arrow across the Welwyn Viaduct and the valley of the Mimram. The looming block on the horizon, to the left of the course of the main line, is surely the great bulk of the Shredded Wheat factory, a green and white art deco(ish) monumental delight which still dominates Welwyn Garden City station today, a constant thumbed nose to the inane 'Howard Centre'. The stations and the districts the two stations served were quite unlike each other and in any case 'Welwyn' was if anything nearer to the village of 'Digswell' and should have been so named. Much of the open country seen in this view has by now succumbed to housing, though there are, if anything, rather more trees, which is a tribute to the maturity of the inhabitants' gardens. The down side (on the right) is much as it was throughout GN days, except for a narrow gauge line which paralleled the siding and curved sharply away to a gas works hidden behind the embankment. This has long gone in this 1940s view. The up side on the other hand, is much altered; that bare strip on the left once had two sidings and there were cattle/sheep pens near to where that upstart hut has appeared. The whole grade of the cutting sides has changed now, and everywhere is heavily wooded; the stonework of the tunnel portal just about peeks out from the surrounding shrubbery.

A Pacific heads south along the great viaduct, 4 April 1938. Welwyn North station is hidden behind its perfect white exhaust; the River Mimram is just visible down on the right.

As rural and as genteelly down-at-heel as any dozing country station – this is the goods yard entrance on the down side in December 1963. Take away the few cars and nothing has really changed in many decades. Certainly a visitor from Great Northern days would recognise his local station.

The goods shed and footbridge on the down side – all, apart from the office extension to the goods shed, period GN structures. The goods shed and loading dock have now disappeared and the bridge cut back so that it serves just the two platforms.

An enchanting little corner of a kind now rarely found. December 1963 was a curious time; all the GN 'infrastructure' was famously still intact (and was to remain so for some years) yet steam was effectively at an end. There was very little traffic left for a goods yard such as this though unprofitable domestic coal (see the wagon and the coalman's sacks) was still being dealt with. Mass commuting and the leaving of cars at stations was also something still to come.

Looking south in December 1963, the viaduct lost in the distance. The down side canopy (on the right) has long disappeared, along with the goods shed and the signal box.

PATRICK STIRLING emerges from South Welwyn tunnel with an up train, in 1958.

The year 1963 was more or less the last gasp (or at least the last gasp could not be far off) of the system whereby wayside stations on the main line provided an all round service, from small packets tied with string to wagonloads of coal, timber or bricks. Peeling, down-at-heel Welwyn North in 1963 typified this time of faded glory and uncertain future – when was the last time you saw three boxes of 'livestock' (day-old chicks maybe, though these usually came in flatter packs...) apparently unattended on a cart on a platform? The main station building is now boarded up though the ticket office below is still manned, and the veranda remains.

The unprepossessing exterior of Welwyn North in 1963. The dreary huts (quite possibly wartime additions – later labelled 'garages') do little to enliven the unlovely prospect. It looks better now, and the trees are still there!

The main station buildings on the up side were extended at times, something which is clear from the new brickwork. The houses on the right, partly visible in some of the other photos, were presumably accommodation for railway staff – they were numbered 1 and 2 in the early 1920s but 19 and 21 by the 1950s. The newer part of the station itself was once a separate cab shed, in days perhaps when the clientele was rather different. By now it was a store and waiting room.

Inside the newer waiting room (on the up side) passengers looked forward to this cosy and welcoming scene. Actually these GN waiting rooms were better than they looked. Hard and bare, they were at least clean and the mean grate (so long as the room was fairly crowded) was welcome enough on a cold morning going to work, when the sun would hardly have risen even when the train reached Kings Cross. By this time of course (1963) the great contrast was the train itself. Ten minutes in the gloom here, collars up and hands deep in pockets, livened only by a flaring and hissing gas lamp were followed by a bright, modern and above all *warm* DMU, flooded in light. Well, sometimes at least – there were also many years to come of the non-corridor steam age stock, hauled by diesels which at this time had yet to shake off a poor reputation, especially for heating failures. Brrrr!

The down side at Welwyn North, December 1963 showing the simple waiting shelter, groaning and leaning a bit with age. Time tends to lend enchantment to such scenes, it is true, but though it would have been the very devil of a place to wait in bad weather (especially given its elevation) the casual intimacy of main line, platform and goods siding/shed beyond must have been some compensation. The faded sign above the entrance to the modest goods shed is the usual ENGINES MUST NOT PASS THIS BOARD. Neither of the platforms were brick by this time, suggesting a renewal of the facings at some period.

The ticket office in 1963. The timber construction of these GN London line stations meant they all had an echoing but muffled quality as the whole thing flexed and moved under the weight of many feet. Yet they absorbed sound so effectively that when passengers were not tramping through they had a peculiarly hushed tone about them. Staff always seemed to appear magically when the passengers came off a train, disappearing again 'for the duration' once the train had left. It was rather like those zoo exhibits where you would stare at the enclosure for ages and never see the occupant, until you doubted anything was there at all...

line station', to include 'new station buildings, platform roofing, footbridge, signal box and other works'.

On Tuesday 5th October 1926 a distinguished party of guests and LNER Officers gathered at the new station, headed by the Rt. Hon. Neville Chamberlain, who was then Minister of Health. It is quite odd to see the pictures of him presiding (in the contemporary *Railway Gazette*) with characteristic moustache, coat, hat and umbrella so fixed in our minds from the time of Munich, over a decade later. By now the garden city had a population of 4,500, so the station, it was considered, had bright prospects – indeed, it was planned that the number of residents should increase no less than ten-fold.

The new station effectively occupied the site of 'Welwyn Junction', its new layout including down goods, down passenger, up passenger and up goods lines. These ran between the two platforms, which served the two slow lines on the main. Loops meant that trains from the fast lines could also call. The two branches, the Luton line on the down side and the Hertford on the up, were served by the outer faces of these platforms. The branches, as mentioned earlier, paralleled the main lines all the way south to Hatfield and the shed there supplied the engines; Welwyn Garden City could now be served both by stopping trains on the main line and by Luton or Hertford branch trains. In 1926 this gave a service of about thirty-seven trains a day, compared with only nine before. It was certainly a notable improvement, and from hereon Welwyn station to the north no longer had the predominance it had previously enjoyed.

At the opening ceremony William Whitelaw, the LNER Chairman, agreed that the change from branch line to main line status would 'open the way for a very great development at Welwyn Garden City.' However, the LNER did not enter lightly upon this project; the company had been criticised for not building a new

A Garden City

A little to the south of Welwyn station beyond the viaduct, two branches, to Hertford and Luton/Dunstable, made connection with (or rather, took their place alongside) the main line at 'Welwyn Junction'. It was an obvious spot for a station but instead both lines ran south, parallel to the main line, two miles or more to Hatfield station, which was effectively the junction station for the two branches. The Hertford line opened in 1858 and for a year or so the Great Northern is said to have had a station of sorts at Welwyn Junction. The Luton line opened in 1860. Both lines had south facing connections with the GN main line and both, it appears, originally connected with it there. It was only a little later, as traffic grew, that both were extended on their separate tracks all the way into Hatfield. The dates of this work was 1869 for the Luton/Dunstable line and 1876 for the Hertford line.

There matters rested until the commuting era began to get under way in the new century. Welwyn Garden City (the place) came into existence after the Great War. Replacing a temporary platform for workmen, a platform with buildings

had opened for the new development on the Dunstable line, a few yards from where it curved away from the course of the main line – this was 'Welwyn Garden City Halt'. Wrottesley also mentions an earlier platform at a similar point on the Hertford line, used only 'specially'. This was a simple wooden platform for workmen, reached by a path across fields and to emphasise that it was barred to the public generally, there was no nameboard. A very good photograph of it appears in *The Hatfield, Luton and Dunstable Railway* by Sue and Geoff Woodward (Oakwood Press, 1994). The development of Welwyn Garden City went on apace and it would not be long before 'Welwyn Garden City Halt' became entirely inadequate. The contract for a new, generously appointed station was duly let to Harold Arnold & Son (who did the new bridge at Peterborough – see *British Railways Illustrated* Vol.5 No.3. and Vol.5 No.4, December 1995 and January 1996). This was on 22 July 1925, though remedial paperwork was still flying about well into the autumn of that year. The price was £23,672 for 'a new main

A most unusual and remarkable photograph. This is the 'Welwyn Garden City Halt', on the line of the Luton/Dunstable branch, though the name board simply says Welwyn Garden City. The area of track is the 'Welwyn Junction' that was and the limitations of the station are clear from this picture – the new town could only be served by trains taking the branch so that, coming from the south, a change was generally necessary at Hatfield. The date is 7 October 1926, though all the signs on the little branch platform are still Great Northern. The new Garden City station, a few yards out of view to the left, had opened two days before, so presumably the old 'halt' was already redundant. The signal is impressive; it is made in concrete and presumably it is its great weight which requires those substantial guy ropes and 'tie posts'.

station even earlier but, Whitelaw pointed out, it had to balance responsibilities to both the public and the shareholders. Since 1 May 1925, the LNER had lost £7,000,000 compared with the previous year.

Neville Chamberlain, it is interesting to note, had called the suburban traffic problem 'insoluble' which is refreshingly honest compared to politicians in later years. Whitelaw clearly saw himself as meeting his

responsibilities by, as he put it, 'doing what he could to ease it'.

By this period the trend of population movement out of central London to the suburbs and outer margins, which continues today, was

A more complete contrast could hardly be imagined; on the same day as the view of the 'halt', 7 October 1926, this is the new station building at Welwyn Garden city. It was in a curious mix of art deco and neo-classical style, then much in vogue for new building on the LNER. The next time you see Neville Chamberlain with that piece of paper, picture him here as Minister of Health, ceremonially drawing a set of curtains to unveil the entrance, and being rewarded with a silver key as a memento.

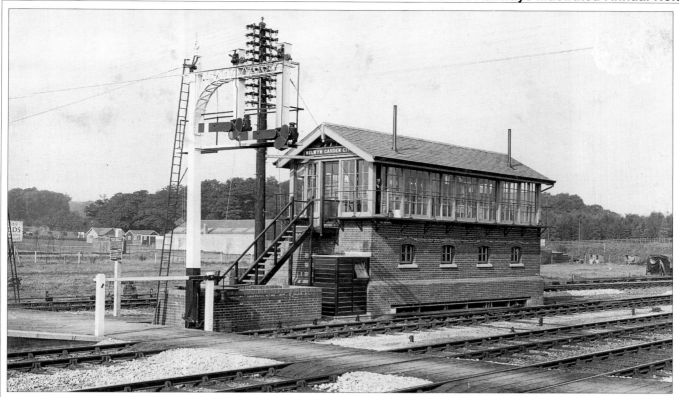

At Welwyn Garden City the station might reflect current architectural mores but signal box design had not changed from the last century. The new box at the north end of the new station, it can be seen, was thoroughly traditional in its building style. The signals are interesting, for they are GN-type 'somersaults' – that is, lower quadrant; note also the barrow crossing, guarded by a counter-weighted barrier.

already a recognised phenomenon. Between 1911 and 1931 the old County of London's population declined from 4,522,000 to 4,397,000 while the 'Outer Ring' (however that was defined) grew from 2,730,000 to 3,806,000. The effect was particularly marked on some parts of the LNER's GN main line – the population of Letchworth, Hitchin and Welwyn Garden City grew 52% (24,594 to 37,421) in just ten years from 1921 to 1931 according to LNER figures now kept at the Public Record Office, Kew. The corresponding growth (though a downturn, the effect of the Great Slump, is evident from 1929) in passenger receipts was as follows:

Year	Hitchin	Letchworth	Welwyn Garden City
1923	£34,368	£24,852	£7,141
1924	£37,260	£25,029	£10,050
1925	£37,307	£25,581	£12,702
1926	£34,507	£22,716	£15,907
1927	£35,584	£24,992	£24,168
1928	£34,930	£26,872	£27,074
1929	£31,559	£26,177	£29,986
1930	£30,988	£25,554	£32,365
1931	£28,360	£23,529	£31,101

A view from the London end of the new station, from the up platform looking north on 7 October 1926. 'An unusual feature', *The Railway Gazette* considered, was the presence on each platform of flower beds. Buildings were all in the local red brick, in the days when we had local brick.

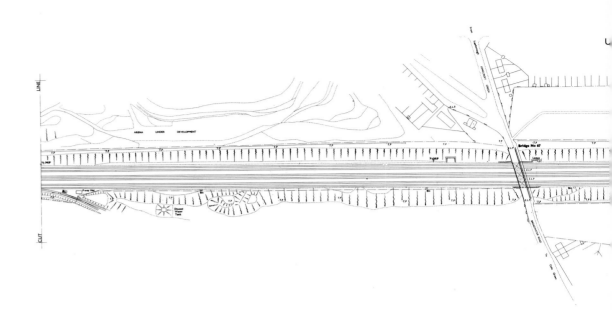

WELWYN GARDEN CITY - BR 1950s PLAN

Economic circumstance was not the only factor in the decline in receipts; Green Line motor coach services were eating into the railway's business by 1931 and by 1932 a drop in receipts of more than 9% was attributed to Green Line buses plying the London-Welwyn Garden City route. The LNER, an internal document of that year records, urgently needed to 'improve the speed and frequency of the service'.

The initial, and somewhat curious, suggestion was for four Sentinel steam railcars having First and Third seats and a toilet, for 88 passengers each, at a cost of over £30,000. The spectacle of steam cars at Kings Cross unfortunately never came to pass and by March 1932 realism had reasserted itself. Two sets of three coaches were found to be spare and it was proposed to utilise these (a Third Brake, Open Third and a

Composite per set) as three coach trains running five services in each direction Kings Cross to Cambridge, with stops at Welwyn Garden City, Hitchin and Letchworth. The only work needed would be 'additional arm rests in the Thirds'. This hurdle was evidently overcome for the service was inaugurated on 2 May 1932. Receipts from Welwyn Garden City, Hitchin and Letchworth were encouraging, after a fashion:

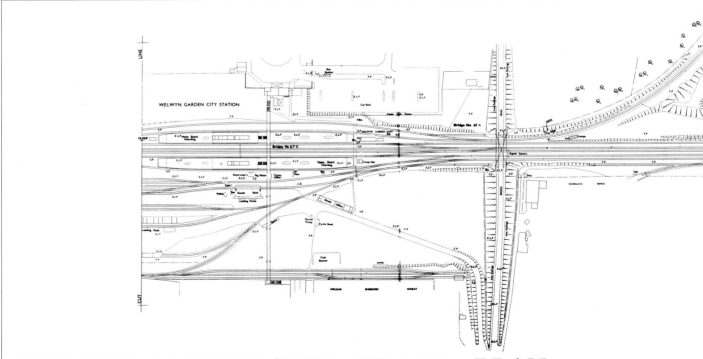

WELWYN GARDEN CITY - BR 1950s PLAN

CT OF WELWYN GARDEN CITY

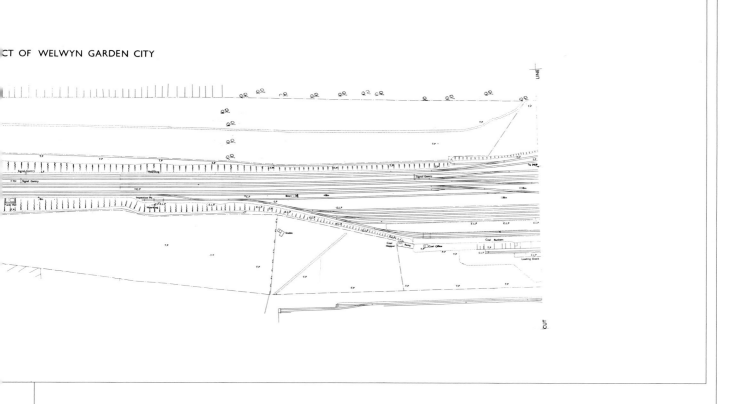

1930-31; £177,698
1931-32; £161,250 (a decrease of 9.3% over previous year)
1932-33; £159,106
Now this last figure was still a decrease it must be admitted, but one of a little over one per cent only. The other stations in the outer suburban service by contrast had managed to see a decline of nearly ten per cent. The special three coach trains, it was declared, had saved

Welwyn Garden City, Hitchin and Letchworth from a similar fate. With buffet profits (as well as the arm rests the two Open Thirds had been fitted with buffets) of £508 the net gain of the whole exercise to the LNER was calculated at £1,734. Together with the rest of the service, the day had evidently been saved.

The goods shed at Welwyn Garden City was not built straight away; tenders indeed were not let

until January 1932. The job went to the aptly named John Bills at £9,757. A report on the desirability of such a facility had been made the previous year, in July 1931 and is illuminating for the light it sheds on the state of affairs at Welwyn Garden City...

Even six years after its opening there was only one LNER siding at Welwyn Garden City, with a capacity of 13 wagons; this was Digswell

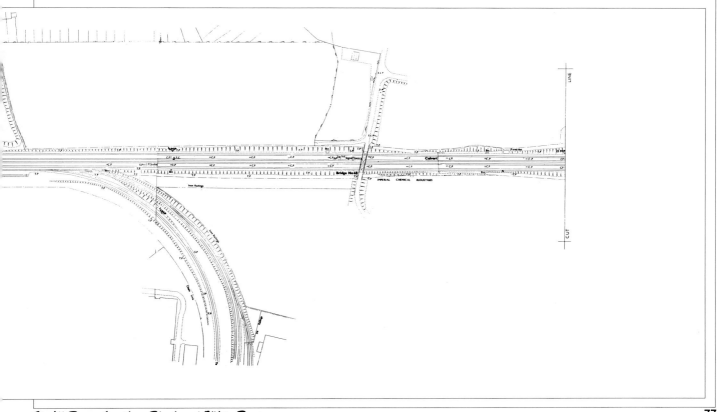

Siding on the line of the Hertford branch, said to have been in existence since 1920 (though it shows on a GN plan of rather earlier than that). Understandably enough, it had 'become inadequate resulting in dissatisfaction among traders generally and the Chamber of Commerce pressing strongly for an immediate improvement'. There was no covered accommodation and carts were dealt with at the station and barrowed across the main lines to the up side to be loaded in the pick-up goods. This was hardly appropriate to a growing garden city; on some nights there were upwards of 150 packages and recourse had to be made to the private sidings belonging to Messrs. Dawnay & Son and the Shredded Wheat Co.'s siding for standing wagons. The Garden City Co.'s siding was also used for dealing with containers and furniture vans and all parties concerned were starting to grumble. With Welwyn Garden City designed ultimately for 50,000 people, the time for a scheme of accommodation had well and truly come. The full scheme proposed was:
(see opposite)

Top. An N7 0-6-2T, No.69637 (presumably one of the Hatfield ones) runs into the goods yard from the north with a freight, almost certainly off the Hertford line, in the 1950s. Photograph MB.

Middle. The general layout of the new station (from the north) with finishing touches being applied on the up platform – almost certainly a bold new hoarding for new houses available locally. The curious arrangement of the footbridge, with its roof as a sort of afterthought and its continuation into a covered way to the station building, is clearly visible. It was later extended across the goods yard to the left, as the text relates, making it a sort of thoroughfare and putting an end to the daily 'mass trespass'.

Bottom. The brand new station building, 7 October 1926. It stood at the eastern end of Howard's Gate, a 200ft wide 'boulevard' unusual for the time in having twin carriageways. In between, in keeping with the garden theme, were well-tended gardens. Howard's Gate led to the Town Square and was intended to be the main shopping and commercial street of the garden city. It would soon be flanked by three storey buildings 'on a consistent architectural theme', and the new station was designed to blend in with this. The station block contained the booking hall and parcels office and even the bicycle store was centrally heated. While the station beyond remains essentially unaltered, this imposing block has gone, entirely subsumed in 'The Howard Centre' – even its foundations have disappeared, with a roadway running beneath. Entrance to the station is now through this modern shopping centre which, in its style, at least bears echoes of that 'consistent architectural theme'.

The down line platform, 7 October 1926. One feature marked out the new station from its fellows on the southern stretch of the GN and that was electric lighting.

Three sidings for 54 wagons in total,
The new goods shed already mentioned, 80ft. long with room for six wagons under cover,
An office for six clerks,
Second-hand 10 ton crane; total cost £11,289.

This does not account for all the sidings eventually provided at the station, so some presumably came later, perhaps in the War, but it is interesting to note just how *much* material could be shifted with even the most basic facilities. The simple Digswell Siding for instance, handled 3,512 tons of goods and 1,765 tons of coal in 1928, rising by 1930 (before the Slump) to 6,071 and 2,343 tons respectively. At its height some years later, the goods yard was shifting so much traffic that trains

were starting there, and an engine pit even had to be provided.

The footbridge at first ran only across the main lines, from one platform to the other, but ultimately had to be extended across the whole of the goods yard and sidings on the up side. It was largely paid for by the Welwyn Garden City UDC, and was designed as 'a public thoroughfare between the east and west sides of the railway'. It cost £6,700 and was built by the Cleveland Bridge and Engineering Co., the tender going to the firm in July 1935. Prior to this inhabitants from the east side were accustomed to simply walk across the ground in between, giving Welwyn Garden City an improbable record, of over a thousand trespassers a day!

All the stations and yards along the GN main line are now of course much altered, in many cases out of all recognition; this *Station Survey* is only intended to portray something of the Welwyns in the steam era and I hope to have succeeded in just that. As the title suggests, it is a 'survey' so that readers can obtain some idea of what the stations looked like in their heyday – well, if not their heyday exactly then how they appeared as working parts of the steam age. I lack the background I'm afraid to put them firmly either in their GN or LNER setting in the sense of workings, track improvements, signalling or even architecture after the fashion of say, the Peter Kay articles in *British Railways Illustrated* and doubtless the GN specialists will groan at some crass omission. I hope I shall be forgiven, and the writings above judged for what they are, a considered but necessarily brief look at two very dissimilar stations serving more or less dissimilar parts of the same small district.
Special thanks to Alec Swain in the compilation of this article.

The station on opening, October 1926. While the buildings and platforms remain, this original bridge has been replaced by a fairly unimpressive modern version. Strangely enough the extension to the bridge (the £6,700 work of 1935 – see text) which of course is not shown here, *does* survive, old and rusty but infinitely more dignified than its modern counterpart. There is even a gate still there, long unused but still ready to deter 'trespassers'. The yard at this time, it can be seen, is entirely undeveloped. All of the background is now occupied by 'The Howard Centre'.

THE ARMY AUXILIARY PIONEER CORPS IN FRANCE

These postcards were issued as a sort of morale raising exercise, with clear propaganda intent and were published in 1939-40. This of course was before the Battle of France was lost and the rather jolly 'wish you were here' mood portrayed disappeared abruptly. Nothing is known of the locations but they illustrate the vital role of railways in war – without them nothing of any bulk could be moved anywhere. Yet in the highly mobile war that was to burst upon the allies, they would become almost valueless. The captions are the original ones on the reverse of the cards themselves, as written by civil servants in the Ministry of Information; wooden and making light of the dangers to come they seem faintly uncomfortable now. At some point, we must remember, these men, many of them veterans of the Great War, would have been overrun by the enemy. Their only escape would have been Dunkirk.

"The Army marches on its stomach" – a very true saying. Men of the Auxiliary Military Pioneer Corps unload flour for the troops and help them march to victory.'

'The same happy, determined spirit which was displayed in 1914 is shown in this photograph of an engine gang of the Auxiliary Pioneer Corps standing on the footplate of an engine.' [The loco is a Dean Goods.]

REAL PHOTOGRAPHS OF THE BRITISH FORCES

BRITISH OFFICIAL POSTCARDS

SET 4 PIONEER CORPS 8 CARDS 1/-

ISSUED BY THE MINISTRY OF INFORMATION
PUBLISHED BY H.M. STATIONERY OFFICE

You'll Remember those White Days...

'Men of the Auxiliary Military Pioneer Corps at work. All types are joining the Corps, and work willingly. The experience which many of the men gained in the last war is of the greatest assistance now.'

'Preparing for the arrival of the new army. Many of these men fought in the last war. Many have sons in the army, but they are still determined to help. These men are constructing army huts.'

You'll Remember those Black and White Days...

'Another job for members of the Auxiliary Military Pioneer Corps. Experience gained by men in civil life is used as much as possible. They are shown here constructing railway sidings.'

"Old Bill" – Auxiliary Military Pioneer Corps version. A veteran of the last war, like many of his comrades, this man is cheerfully helping once more. He is controlling a winch.'

WAR REPORT ... WAR REPORT ... WAR R

'Men of the Auxiliary Military Pioneer Corps are now 'doing their bit' in France. Their work is of great value and they do it with a will. They are shown here unloading a ship.'

'The Auxiliary Military Pioneer Corps is primarily to "make the wheels go round". Jobs are many and varied. Here is a group of men loading a railway truck "Somewhere in France".'
(Material courtesy Alec Swain and 'certified genuine by the Wembley Lion Appreciation Society, 31 May 1995'. Are there any readers who served in the Corps, and have any readers seen other wartime cards like the ones here?)

You'll Remember those Black and White Days...

Two Scots on E

By the early months of 1963 main line passenger steam out of Euston was in headlong retreat but there were still stirring sights to be seen, in between the endless EE Type 4s. On 16 March 1963 46156 THE SOUTH WALES BORDERER ran north through rain on the Down Fast, taking water and losing a fair bit of it over the back the tender. This was the first opportunity to refill after leaving London and seldom missed, for Euston did not have platform end columns and a loco probably had not taken water since it left Camden shed, or hour or more, maybe, before departing north. Photographs J.G. Walmsley, The Transport Treasury.

You'll Remember those Black and White Days...

ushey Troughs

A few weeks later, on 20 April 1963 (the trees just beginning to come into spring leaf) 46165 THE RANGER (12th LONDON REGT.) came north on the Down Fast with a train of parcels van, taking water as usual. Crews habitually took water whenever the opportunity arose, whatever the level in the tender (well, almost) and the need to have plenty in reserve was drummed into everyone. Poor old 46165 is in grimy state, reflecting its relegation from top flight work. The 'fan' of water thrown up by the scoop is visible in the lower picture, separating as it hits the brake cross rodding. Photographs J.G. Walmsley, The Transport Treasury.

No Smoke Without Fire...

Now there's exhaust, and there's exhaust... On that same miserable day in the winter of 1963-64 this glorious northbound ensemble roared by Camden shed – that's the staff footbridge over to Camden Goods a few yards away. 46245 CITY OF LONDON was in its last full year of life, and it is tempting to conclude that the Black Five in front is the Rugby pilot, returning home. The number unfortunately is just impossible to see, even with a powerful glass but the Pacific would probably not need the extra power; 'putting one on front' was the easiest way to get an engine and, more crucially, the crew, back north without complication. Photographs J.G. Walmsley, The Transport Treasury.

The flat topped hills, capped with hard millstone grit, proclaim this to be the Settle and Carlisle; Milepost 260 in fact, just north of Ais Gill. 92023 plods along with what looks like stone hoppers, a heavy unyielding load which fortunately has led to these marvellous smoke effects – the sort photographers might pay money for today.

You'll Remember those Black and White Days...

Impressive smoke effects from 8F 48365 coming up Camden Bank in horrible weather in 1963 – or perhaps it's early 1964. These are the empty carriage lines, with Camden shed a few yards away behind the photographer. The 2-8-0 is certainly making a song and dance of it, though it's impossible to see if it has a load behind or not. It's wet, and it's cold.

RAILWAYS OF THE BUCHAN AREA

BUC

a - PHILORTH
(Private station)
b - KIRKTON BRIDGE
HALT
c - PHILORTH BRIDGE
HALT

FRASERBURGH

b
CAIRNBULG
a
c
ST. COMBS

RATHEN

LONMAY

MORMOND

STRICHEN

N

BRUCKLAY

INVERUGIE

MAUD
JUNCTION
MINTLAW
LONGSIDE
NEWSEAT
PETERHEAD

BODDAM

AUCHNAGATT
LONGHAVEN

CRUDEN BAY
BULLERS O'BUCHAN
HATTON
PLATFORM

ARNAGE
PITLURG

AUCHMACOY

ELLON

ESSLEMONT

LOGIERIEVE

UDNY

NEW MACHAR

*to Keith
and Inverness*
NORTH
SEA

PARKHILL

(For clarity, minor stations
south of Dyce are not
represented)
DYCE

KITTYBREWSTER
Waterloo
(Goods)
ABERDEEN

to Ballater

to Dundee

0   4   8 miles

The Great North of Scotland Railway reached Mintlaw on the Buchan section on 18 July 1861 and was extended to Peterhead on 3 July the following year. A branch from Maud Junction arrived in Fraserburgh on 24 April 1865. It was a further 38 years and with the help of the 'Light Railways' Act, before a branch from

Notes by Bryan Wilson

Fraserburgh to St Combs was completed, for operation on and from 1 July 1903. Fraserburgh itself was

a dead end terminal station and the St Combs branch ran in a south easterly direction from the terminus. Michael Bland was lucky enough to travel these lines on 4 September 1958 and his record has enabled us to re-live the journeys. A few 'extras' from the same camera help us on our way towards Aberdeen.

AN AND BEYOND

LM 2-6-0 No.46460 which went to Kittybrewster shed in January 1952 waits at Fraserburgh on 4 September 1958 with the 10.30am branch train to St Combs. It has the mandatory cowcatcher as much of the branch was unfenced. In earlier days, J91 and J90 0-6-0 tanks held sway, until they were replaced by North British D51 4-4-0Ts in June 1926. This type lasted for seven years until April 1933, when Great Eastern F4s, surplus with the closure of the Gifford branch, took over and remained in everyday charge until 1952. Although cowcatchers were specified and normally provided, the odd D40 4-4-0 still worked on the branch when 'needs must'. 46460 and its train is in the St Combs platform at Fraserburgh, provided when the station was rebuilt from a simple two platform station at the turn of the century. That familiar phrase is now unfortunately lost to us of course – we have to say now 'about 1900' which is something of a loss! When it opened, the St Combs branch was controlled by a ground frame released by 'Annetts Key' until a new signal box opened on 2 August 1904. The points at Cairnbulg and St Combs were also controlled by Annetts Key. There were no signals on the branch itself. Returning to the photograph, on the left LMS 2P No.40650 waits to make a shunt. We shall see more of this loco as the day progresses. There seems to be more activity in the adjacent Goods Yard than on the platform. Photograph M. Bland, The Transport Treasury.

Left. 40650 with the tower of Dalrymple Hall behind it, making a shunt before departing south later on with a freight train. As late in the branch's life as this is, there were still three regular fish services from Fraserburgh daily. 40650 came north in the spring of 1948 (with 40603 and 40622) as a first effort to replace GNoS D40/41s and NBR D31s working north of Aberdeen. Like all 'imports' they were unpopular with the local enginemen and in early years spent a lot of time on local goods and livestock workings. They did however, stand the test of time and remained (strengthened by further arrivals of the class) until the end of steam at Kittybrewster. 40650 then moved 'on paper' to Ferryhill, to be condemned a month later and cut up at Inverurie. The 'fishy business' is on the train of Conflat 'A's on the left. Photograph M. Bland, The Transport Treasury.

Below left. Philorth Bridge Halt, opened with the branch, was a 'request' stop. An ash and cinder platform held in place by timber baulks suffices, with the mandatory coach body for shelter. Bicycles were still an important way of getting around in the far North East in 1958 (when harvesting was still conducted in the traditional way) and could safely be left by the station. In the days before general car ownership (and the roads to drive them on) it is difficult to comprehend now just how remote some parts of Scotland, Wales and England, come to that, were just a few decades ago. Photograph M. Bland, The Transport Treasury.

Below. On the way back, showing the unfenced character of the line – hence the requirement for cowcatchers. The van on the road is SOY 79 of July 1957, thus 'nearly new' and belonging to the Singer Sewing Machine Co of Union Street Aberdeen. A desolate spot, the nearest town was Fraserburgh. Photograph M. Bland, The Transport Treasury.

You'll Remember those Black and White Days...

The terminus at St Combs with some custom in evidence at least. The run round siding on the left was controlled by Annetts Key on the train staff. This is a real 'modeller's' view of the cowcatcher. 46460 went on to Keith in May 1960, Eleven months after the branch had been dieselised. Photograph M. Bland, The Transport Treasury.

Running into Fraserburgh. A good view of the place, with the old United Free church on the left a rather grand and imposing sight. The two road shed in granite adjoins the platform, from which there were four steps down into the yard. The Standard 2-6-4 tank is 80114 which arrived at Kittybrewster in April 1957 until it moved to Keith in October 1960. These locos were used on the Buchan and Deeside lines as well as on locals between Aberdeen and Inverurie. The turntable is behind the tank engine. Poking its nose out behind the coal wagon is 40650. And the fish still waits. Photograph M. Bland, The Transport Treasury.

Having dealt with Fraserburgh and St Combs our photographer Mr Bland returned south to Maud Junction behind 80114 which is looking a bit scruffy. These standard tanks never received the normal attention associated with Kittybrewster shed. The Peterhead line can be seen going off right under the footbridge steps. Manson tablet exchange apparatus was provided at passing points on the line but the BR tanks soon lost the catchers, due to the awkwardness of dealing with them from the side window cab. Note the LMS stock – this had replaced LNER vehicles from 1955 onwards. Photograph M. Bland, The Transport Treasury.

Mr Bland has now arrived at Peterhead (having left 80114 to continue to Aberdeen) to find BR Standard Class 2 2-6-0 No.78045 waiting in the platform. This loco came new to Kittybrewster in October 1955 and stayed until transfer to Keith in June 1960. The post office van SLO 479 of 1956 is certainly a 'period piece'. Peterhead also boasted a two road granite engine shed and a turntable, sited in the goods yard. There was also a branch to the harbour, which included a private siding to the slaughterhouse. Mr Bland then joined the service to Maud Junction where 78045 left the train to attach a further vehicle or vehicles. Photograph M. Bland, The Transport Treasury.

You'll Remember those Black and White Days...

78045 entering the yard at Maud Junction. Cattle pens in two places indicate the importance of livestock here. This view clearly shows the parting of the ways, left to Fraserburgh, right to Peterhead. Maud had a privately owned Refreshment Room that survived, peculiarly, after withdrawal of the passenger service. The station had North and South signal boxes until 21 July 1935 when 'Maud Junction' took over the whole station area, until 5 March 1969. To add insult to local injury, this was a North British Type 8 Box! The main signal reading in the wrong direction from the down Fraserburgh platform enabled Peterhead portions to be detached and set back for running round purposes, or for trains to terminate and return towards Aberdeen. The 'running in' board on the Peterhead platform read 'Maud change for Fraserburgh', even if you were in a portion of a train which arrived on that side and were in fact being detached and worked forward with no changing. Photograph M. Bland, The Transport Treasury.

Continuing south from Maud involved a stop at Ellon, junction for passengers to Boddam to October 1932 (freight lasted some more years, to November 1945). The station nameboard in former years read 'Ellon Jn for Cruden Bay', the *Cruden Bay Hotel* of the GNoS being the attraction. 40650 from Fraserburgh has beaten us here with its pick up freight. It had that same headcode on, remember, in the morning and confirms reports of the work these locos did in the area. Inevitably, some fish containers constituted part of the load. Those water columns repay a second look, while the signalman walks to our loco with the tablet for the single line section to Udny. Passenger services to Peterhead came to an end on 3 May 1965 as did the line from Fraserburgh to St Combs. Fraserburgh itself survived that summer, closing on 4 October 1965. Goods traffic continued to Peterhead until 7 September 1970 and to Fraserburgh until 8 October 1979. Photograph M. Bland, The Transport Treasury. *Thanks to the Great North of Scotland Railway Association for help in compiling these notes.*

ENDPIECE
Intimate Portrait of a Pannier Tank

A poor old tired 8743, not long for this BR world, stands in Old Oak Common roundhouse in the early 1960s. Wonderful battered detail for the modeller – the sandbox behind the step with its lid in the cut-out, the knocked-about edges and the stains and corrosion and dirt. Even the toecap scuffs on the paint by the footsteps. Marvellous stuff! That's the ATC shoe beneath the buffer beam – not an item we often get a good look at. We'll leave you with the chalked comment, obviously done by a *British Railways Illustrated* proof reader: ENGEINE WANT'S COALING.

You'll Remember those Black and White Days...